You Are What You Read

SKILLS FOR SCHOLARS

You Are What You Read

A Practical Guide to Reading Well

Robert DiYanni

PRINCETON UNIVERSITY PRESS

Princeton and Oxford

Requests for permission to reproduce material from this work should be sent to permissions@press.princeton.edu

Published by Princeton University Press
41 William Street, Princeton, New Jersey 08540
99 Banbury Road, Oxford OX2 6JX

press.princeton.edu

First paperback printing, 2022
Paperback ISBN 978-0-691-20677-6

The Library of Congress has cataloged the cloth edition of this book as follows:

Names: DiYanni, Robert, author.
Title: You are what you read : a practical guide to reading well / Robert DiYanni.
Description: Princeton : Princeton University Press, [2021] | Includes bibliographical references and index.
Identifiers: LCCN 2020029863 (print) | LCCN 2020029864 (ebook) | ISBN 9780691206783 (hardback) | ISBN 9780691216607 (epub)
Subjects: LCSH: Reading. | Literature—Appreciation.
Classification: LCC PN83 .D59 2021 (print) | LCC PN83 (ebook) | DDC 418/.4—dc23
LC record available at https://lccn.loc.gov/2020029863
LC ebook record available at https://lccn.loc.gov/2020029864

British Library Cataloging-in-Publication Data is available

Editorial: Peter Dougherty and Alena Chekanov
Production Editorial: Lauren Lepow
Text Design: Pamela L. Schnitter
Jacket/Cover design: Matt Avery (Monograph LLC)
Production: Erin Suydam
Publicity: Alyssa Sanford and Kathryn Stevens

This book has been composed in Verdigris MVB Pro text, Aktiv Grotesk, Miller

For Ruth and Keira Ruth,
who share a love of reading

It's the books,

the reading that can change one's life.

I'm the living evidence.

—Sean Connery

Contents

Preface

The title of this book can be taken literally. We *are* what we read. While every individual is unique, all of us possess unlimited potential. Eat well and you will be healthier. Exercise well and you will be stronger. Read well and you will be . . . what? Smarter? Maybe. More informed? Surely. But this book is not about those things. This book suggests that in reading well you will be more alive.

Reading well awakens and broadens the mind. It provides a vast realm of inner experience that extends far beyond everyday life. Reading well, you will still be you. But you will be a better and more interesting version of yourself.

My aim in this book is to present varied approaches to the deeply gratifying experience of reading, especially reading literature. These strategies can lead to thought-provoking and emotionally resonant textual encounters. *You Are What You Read* celebrates reading's value for learning and for living. It presents ways to enrich your reading practices and enhance your reading pleasure.

This is not a theoretical book, but a practical one, its aim to improve a reader's understanding and appreciation of literature. It's intended for anyone interested in getting more out of reading and more out of life. The brief discussions of theory in the book's later chapters illuminate the benefits of reading. I present just enough theory to enhance literary discernment, deepen literary understanding, and increase literary pleasure.

My major claim is that learning to read confidently and skillfully enhances our lives and helps us enjoy life more completely. This enjoyment stems from honing our powers of observation and enhancing our capacity for thinking well. I believe, in short, that we can attain better lives through reading.

We read with multiple goals—for information, enjoyment, self-gratification, self-advancement; to be instructed, entertained, moved, inspired. We read to understand and appreciate, to grow and develop. *You Are What You Read* attempts to help readers achieve these goals.

The rewards of reading are especially important today, a time of complex challenges we are all confronting. Economic turbulence has combined with frightening uncertainties and inexorable ambiguities. These disturbing realities are inflected across a spectrum of recent and ongoing catastrophes, from the Covid-19 pandemic to climate change, with extreme forms of weather cascading in ever-longer droughts along with wilder and more destructive fires and floods; from the global political and economic crises of mass migration and unemployment to individual and social problems—crippling addictions, surges in stress and anxiety, dramatic upheavals in education and social services—all exacerbated by the Covid-19 crisis and the inescapable changes that accompany it.

Reading well—with skill and confidence, even expertise—matters now more than ever. Reading literature with understanding and pleasure can help us navigate the myriad disruptions we are living through. Reading won't solve life's increasingly intractable problems, but it can provide perspective on them and relief from them. Reading well can help us better understand the challenges we face together and help ameliorate the pain and suffering we endure. It can also take our minds off them for a while.

The value of learning to read well lies in the manifold pleasures it brings, the knowledge it affords, and the imaginative enlargement of life it yields. Learning to read well and to enjoy better reading is not as hard as most people think. Each of the book's chapters recommends ways to achieve this seemingly ambitious goal. Each illustrates how reading heightens our appreciation of living.

Taken together, the six chapters present a suite of interrelated, mutually reinforcing strategies for reading well.

- Chapter 1 focuses on listening. It argues that seeking textual meaning *first and foremost* yields far less value than what happens when we resist pouncing on "meaning" and, instead, begin by asking what texts *say* and *suggest*, what they *show* and *do*.

- Chapter 2 poses and answers two questions: "What truths do texts tell?" "How might we read for those textual truths"?
- Chapters 3 and 4 demonstrate how we can engage works of nonfiction and fiction productively and pleasurably.
- Chapter 5 contextualizes practical applications of reading with a bit of theory. It considers reading's paradoxical pleasures via the dialectical energies that impel and enliven the reading of literature.
- Chapter 6 draws out the implications reading literature can have for living life more rewardingly. In tandem with chapter 5, it recapitulates the book's major themes and underscores the entwining of reading and living.

I've included a short coda that recommends nine reading practices that can enhance the experience of any reader. Appendixes A and B identify benefits and drawbacks of print and digital reading, and propose recommendations for what to read and why.

You Are What You Read participates in a long-standing conversation with writers and readers past and present. Reading literature gives us access to the multitude of voices that constitute that conversation. You can banter in the trenches under fire in a world war, fall in love again (and get it right this time), experience the brutality of slavery, voyage to the moon or the center of the earth, dive deep into the human mind and heart.

This life-affirming and life-enhancing conversation has been going on for millennia. I invite you, as a singular reader, to join in. Bring your thoughts and feelings, your ideas and personal values. Take your place in the conversation so that reading well can, indeed, help you attain a fuller and more rewarding life.

PART ONE Approaches

ONE Reading and Questioning

WHAT TEXTS SAY AND SUGGEST

WHAT THEY SHOW AND DO—AND HOW

Reading sets our minds, our inquiring minds, in
motion as we pursue a deeper understanding
of our lives and the world we live in.
—PAT C. HOY II

An important question readers consider when reading literature
and other challenging texts is "What does the text mean?" It's a familiar question, and it no doubt stimulates thoughtful inquiry.
I'm not ready to abandon it. However, I think we should consider
its limitations for literary understanding, especially its interference
with readers' enjoyment of literature. To think about the question
of meaning productively, we need to postpone it and reframe it in
the context of other textual considerations. Reading for meaning
is important, but it shouldn't drive our reading practices and limit
our reading pleasures.

What other questions might we ask about what we read? What
else can we consider about a text, while postponing the quest for
meaning? Though grappling with textual meaning(s) may be our
ultimate goal, it does not follow that we should *begin* with the question of meaning. Other questions can lead us into, around, and
through texts, literary works especially, with enhanced pleasure
and understanding.

The questions we ask about texts reflect fundamental assumptions about textual understanding, about interpretation. Our
questions determine the directions our reading can take. Our
questions determine what we are able to see and say about texts;
they profoundly influence how we perceive texts and what we
make of them. Changing our questions changes both our understanding of texts, literary works especially, and the value they
hold for us.

Let's consider, to start, a brief essay by Yoshida Kenko, a fourteenth-century Japanese writer. Kenko was a Buddhist monk best known for his *Essays in Idleness*, among the most studied of Japanese literary works, a book that remains today a staple of the Japanese high school curriculum. The following essay, like all of Kenko's essays, carries a number as its title.

Essay 189

You may intend to do something today, only for pressing business to come up unexpectedly and take up all of your attention the rest of the day. Or a person you have been expecting is prevented from coming, or someone you hadn't expected comes calling. The thing you have counted on goes amiss, and the thing you had no hopes for is the only one to succeed. A matter which promised to be a nuisance passes off smoothly, and a matter which should have been easy proves a great hardship. Our daily experiences bear no resemblance to what we had anticipated. This is true throughout the year, and equally true for our entire lives. But if we decide that everything is bound to go contrary to our anticipations, we discover that naturally there are also some things which do not contradict expectations. This makes it all the harder to be definite about anything. The one thing you can be certain of is the truth that all is uncertainty.

Refusing to say what his essay is about, Kenko leaves us to decide this for ourselves. He draws us into the essay's topic without naming it first. Instead, we dive right into the situation—ways our intentions get subverted. Eventually, by the end, Kenko states his claim: the one thing we can be certain of is uncertainty.

How does Kenko manage this topic? How does he carry us along his trail of thought? How does he engage us in thinking along with him? He does these things by making our reading experience inductive. Kenko provides examples, but he withholds the idea those examples illustrate—until the end.

He also engages us personally. From the opening word, "You," Kenko addresses us directly. He speaks to us, naturally, even informally, "you" and "your" appearing six times in the first three sentences. The fourth sentence, using no pronouns at all, serves as a hinge, a fulcrum. From there the passage pivots to the first-person plural: Kenko talks of "our" experiences, "our" lives, and "our anticipations"; he mentions things "we discover" about our everyday experience. The move is from the individual to the larger group, from the particular "you" to the more general "we."

The essay's brevity is also noteworthy: a single paragraph of nine sentences and fewer than 175 words. In that short space Kenko invites us to consider the ways our lives are replete with the incidental and accidental. He alludes to how plans become disrupted, intentions circumvented, the way things go awry. Not always, however, as he notes that some things do go the way we hope or expect. Kenko reminds us that we don't know and can't know which things will work out for us and which will not. Uncertainty sabotages our confidence.

Kenko's essay operates on a fairly high level of generality, his examples notwithstanding. The essay's personal tone and informal style coexist with declarative sentences that remain general, nonspecific. Kenko offers us nothing about his personal experience. Instead, he gets us thinking more broadly about uncertainty, about the indefinite, and about our inability to control events. Implicitly, Kenko invites us to apply his general assertions to our own experience; we reflect on our own personal examples to substantiate, qualify, or perhaps challenge his claims.

Genre

One question we need to ask when encountering a text is what kind of text it seems to be. Just what are we looking at (and listening to)? Though brief, Kenko's text makes clear that it's an essay—a considered set of observations about human experience. And we respond to essays differently from the ways we respond to fictional works or to poems or plays. Essays make different demands on us than do works in other literary genres.

Here is another short prose text, considerably briefer than Kenko's mini-essay. What might we make of its mere two sentences?

> This is just to say I have eaten the plums that were in the icebox and which you were probably saving for breakfast. Forgive me, they were delicious so sweet and so cold.

This text appears to be an explanatory note, a weak apology, one that might be attached to a refrigerator door. Its matter-of-fact tone, its seeking of forgiveness (playfully and teasingly), and its speaker's pleasure in eating the plums suggest as much. But what if these words were rearranged as their author, William Carlos Williams, published them?

THIS IS JUST TO SAY

I have eaten
the plums
that were in
the icebox

and which
you were probably
saving
for breakfast

Forgive me
they were delicious
so sweet
and so cold

How does our experience of reading this version of the text, as verse, differ from our experience reading it as a prose note of apology? How does our response to the text change when aligned as the poem Williams wrote? Seeing those sentences spanning the margins of a page, we understand them one way—as an everyday note.

Seeing them lineated as a poem, we approach and *experience* them differently—as literature. The change in genre alters our perspective and our *perception*—how we take what we are reading, what we make of it, and what we do with it. The shift of genre from note to poem changes all this and more.

Williams's poem slows down our reading, focusing our attention on plums swiped from the icebox that someone else was anticipating eating for breakfast—these facts, along with a description of their taste and the physical sensation of eating them. It's not that those details were unavailable in the prose apology— but rather that they were not accentuated and brought to our attention the way they are in Williams's poem.

Once we accept a text *as* a literary work, we know better how to look at it, what to do with it; we know what questions to ask of it and what kinds of analysis to subject it to. We know what rewards such attention can yield. Genre knowledge guides our reading of literary works; knowing a text's genre is crucial for understanding it.

Applying the conventions of literary analysis to bumper stickers, shopping lists, advertisements for shampoo, and other mundane texts is possible, of course, but the payoff is far less than when those conventions are applied to an epigram by Martial or Pope, or a lyric by Wordsworth or Dickinson—to say nothing of grander works, such as "Ode on a Grecian Urn," *The Tempest, Jane Eyre, The Fire Next Time,* or *One Hundred Years of Solitude.* Why? Because each of those literary works says much more; each shows more, does more, suggests more, signifies more, and does so with greater complexity and fecundity.

Contexts

Considerations of context beyond genre can open up a text in still other ways. We can ask about the relationship of the text to its author's other works. How, for example, does the speaker eating plums in "This Is Just to Say" compare with the speaker eating plums in another of Williams's poems, "To a Poor Old Woman"? How are those speaker's acts of plum eating different?

Or, alternatively, how does Williams's emphasis in "To a Poor Old Woman" differ from his emphasis in "This Is Just to Say?" To what does "To a Poor Old Woman" direct our attention?

To a Poor Old Woman

munching a plum on
the street a paper bag
of them in her hand

They taste good to her
They taste good
to her. They taste
good to her

You can see it by
the way she gives herself
to the one half
sucked out in her hand

Comforted
a solace of ripe plums
seeming to fill the air
They taste good to her

We notice first how the title is part of the poem's opening description: it provides a point of view—how things taste to the poor old woman. We likely notice the sheer joy and sensuous pleasure the woman takes in eating those plums; we see how they comfort her; we feel the solace they bring her. We also notice how Williams plays with line endings to shift the emphasis at the end of lines from the woman ("her") eating the plums, to their "good" taste, and her particular pleasure in eating them. The repetition of the full line at the end of the poem closes it up and reemphasizes just how good those plums tasted, calling up, perhaps, the "sweet" taste and "cold" touch of the plums in "This Is Just to Say."

We notice as well, especially when we read the poem aloud, how Williams directs our attention to the way the poor old woman eats the plums, sucking out half at a time. The poem pushes toward two key words that complement these concrete details—"Comforted" and "solace"—abstract words that convey what her eating of the plums gives her.

Similarity and difference; similarity but difference. Connections and distinctions. We read poems and other literary works in relation to one another. We read everything in context.

We now slow down a bit to consider Williams's famous poem about a red wheelbarrow:

THE RED WHEELBARROW

so much depends
upon

a red wheel
barrow

glazed with rain
water

beside the white
chickens

What, we might ask ourselves, does this poem have in common with the others? Though there are no plums in the wheelbarrow, "The Red Wheelbarrow" shares characteristics with Williams's poems about plums: everyday subjects, simple language, short lines, a lack of end rhyme. The poems' appearance on the page, their visual form, directs us how to read them; their form influences how we see, hear, and take them, and what we make of them.

Describing "The Red Wheelbarrow" without worrying, initially, about its meaning frees us to notice patterns of sound and structure (as for example the assonance of lines 5 and 7 (glazed with rain; beside the white), and the use of two-line stanzas, with the first line containing three words and the second line a single word of two-syllables). We can notice those things upon a second look and hearing. We can detect patterns, make connections, ask questions, consider values the work embodies, and arrive at a provisional sense of the poem's significance. In looking carefully at its stanzas, for example, we might see each as a miniature wheelbarrow.

Another striking feature of the poem is the way Williams breaks its lines, where he turns each. By splitting "upon" from "what depends," Williams provokes us to wonder "What depends?" And, perhaps, "Why does it depend?" The word "depends" means literally "to hang from." And that is just what the word "upon" does in the poem: it hangs from the first line: "so much depends." It hangs there for us to see; and it hangs there, too, for us to think about.

In the second and third stanzas, Williams breaks lines over the words "wheelbarrow" and "rainwater." Why might he have done that and with what effect(s)? One possibility for "wheel" / "barrow" is that Williams reminds us (and helps us see) that a wheelbarrow is an object made of two parts—a "barrow" on "wheel"(s). Similarly, Williams emphasizes the fact that "rainwater" is indeed "water" that "rain(s)" down from the sky. He accomplishes this by visually dividing the words across lines on the page. In making those divisions, he gets us looking at words and noticing the things those words refer to. In the process, we see both the words and the things they describe anew.

Seeing one poem in the context of others aids what we can see and say about each. In addition to contextualizing poems and other literary works in relationship to one another, we can also consider them in the contexts of an author's life and milieu.

Contexts: Life and World

A signal fact about William Carlos Williams is that he embedded his writing life in his work as a busy pediatrician practicing in Rutherford, New Jersey. Lacking much time to write, he often jotted notes and lines of poems between his appointments with patients. And though Williams did write one long epic poem, *Paterson*, his oeuvre leans heavily toward short stories, essays, and lyric poems. Given his circumstances, this isn't surprising.

Beyond the context of an author's life per se, we might consider how a writer's works reflect, embody, or otherwise relate to the larger world in which that life was lived. We might consider, that is, any particular text in light of the cultural milieu in which it was created. Contexts of work, life, and world allow us to expand our relationship with any particular text, enlarging our understanding of its implications and increasing our appreciation of its value. We might imagine these three contextual relationships as concentric circles: the individual text radiating into the larger contexts of a writer's oeuvre, the writer's life, and the writer's milieu.

We can illustrate with Flannery O'Connor, whose works, mostly short stories, embody an ironic vision, one embedded in the genre, temper, and spirit of Southern Gothic. O'Connor's identity as a southerner provided her with many of the raw materials she used to construct the nuanced settings of her stories and invent their richly imagined characters. Born in Savannah, Georgia, and living most of her adult life in Milledgeville, Georgia, the state's capital before the Civil War, O'Connor found her métier in portraying the South in all its complexity. Her stories, with their grotesque characters, frequent violence, savage satire, and colloquial dialogue, often point to the comic in calamity, while exploring moral issues in imaginative and provocative ways.

Complementing O'Connor's sense of herself as a southerner was her Roman Catholic faith. Her religious beliefs provide a way in to her fiction, though we need not share her beliefs to enjoy her stories. Belief is not required for appreciation.

We can see its centrality in her best-known story, "A Good Man Is Hard to Find," in which an escaped convict comes into contact with a family traveling on vacation. Here is its opening paragraph:

> The grandmother didn't want to go to Florida. She wanted to visit some of her connections in east Tennessee and she was seizing at every chance to change Bailey's mind. Bailey was the son she lived with, her only boy. He was sitting on the edge of his chair at the table, bent over the orange sports section of the *Journal*. "Now look here, Bailey," she said, "see here, read this," and she stood with one hand on her thin hip and the other rattling the newspaper at his bald head. "Here this fellow that calls himself The Misfit is aloose from the Federal Pen and headed toward Florida and you read here

what it says he did to these people. Just you read it. I wouldn't take my children in any direction with a criminal like that aloose in it. I couldn't answer to my conscience if I did." (137)

The story is set in the American Southeast. That the narrator refers to the grandmother's relatives as "connections" indicates the character's sense of status, suggesting her imagined gentility. In referring to her son as "her only boy" and as "the son she lived with," the narrator reveals their domestic arrangement and her babying of him. The word "boy" for this adult male will echo later in the story for the grandmother when she calls out "Bailey Boy," after she hears a sharp pistol shot emanating from the woods, where the family, in a car accident, encounters the grandmother's nemesis, "The Misfit." O'Connor hints at, but does not identify exactly, what "he [the Misfit] did to these people" about whom the grandmother was reading as she was "rattling" the newspaper at her son's bald head. (Notice how each of these details suggests an aspect of the son's or the grandmother's character, efficiently yet humorously, while also creating, ominously, the first hint of the danger they will later confront.)

The grandmother's use of the word "aloose" comically identifies her lack of linguistic sophistication. The word also reveals how she manipulates her son by trying to frighten him with the highly unlikely possibility that they would encounter The Misfit in a state the size of Florida. But, of course, this is a short story by Flannery O'Connor, and so we suspect that this paragraph presages the encounter the grandmother fears, however unlikely it might be in everyday life.

O'Connor incorporates a number of religious elements in her story. Among the most important are the details The Misfit shares about his life: "I never was a bad boy that I remember of . . . but somewheres along the line I done something wrong and got sent to the penitentiary. I was buried alive" (149). We learn more when he says to the grandmother, "You can do one thing or you can do another, kill a man or take a tire off his car, because sooner or later you're going to forget what it was you done and just be punished for it" (150). And further: "I call myself The Misfit . . . because I can't make what all I done wrong fit what all I gone through in punishment. . . . Does it seem right to you, lady, that one is punished a heap and another ain't punished at all?" (151). The Misfit links these ruminations and questions with Jesus, who he says "thown everything off balance. It was the same case with Him as with me except He hadn't committed any crime" (151).

The Misfit's frustration at not knowing whether Jesus really was a miracle worker, a divine being who raised the dead and raised himself from the dead, leads him to his view that in life there is "[n]o pleasure but meanness" (152) and "[i]t's no real pleasure in life" (153). The logic of the Misfit's explanation helps us understand his view of life. It is at once harshly realistic and steadily unconventional, while also being consonant with O'Connor's Christian theological paradigm.

In considering a work in different contexts, including genre, life, and milieu, we expand our understanding of it, and also of the literary ur-question we began with. In a sense, we have been questioning this question about itself, testing its limitations and exploring alternative variations on it.

Meaning, Saying, Doing

Let's turn now to some further variations of our initial question. In addition to "What does the text *mean?*" we can also ask, "What does the text *say?*" and "What does the text *do?*" Now this first variation sounds much like our question about meaning. But we can use this *saying* version of it, instead, to focus attention on voice, to attend to the tone of the speaker's words and to the attitude conveyed by that tone. Asking what the text *says* invites us to listen to its voice(s). Attending to voice in a text helps us develop an ear for how it sounds, especially if we read it aloud.

Why might we want to do this?

Attending to a texts's aural dimension, privileging its sounds, leads to an appreciation for the music of prose and poetry, rhythm especially. Developing an auditory imagination increases our ability to hear the rhythms of good writing and to feel its pulse, thereby adding to our reading pleasure.

Taking another tack, we can observe that reading aloud enables writers to hear infelicities in their prose that they normally don't see on the silent page. The ear hears what the eye overlooks; the ear prompts the eye to see. Reading aloud enables writers and readers to hear how sound shapes sense.

Reading aloud offers other advantages, as well. Readers must make choices about the tempo and tone of their reading. They must choose a spirit in which to read, one that allows the rhythms of word and phrase, sentence and paragraph, to reveal the shape of thought. The skills resulting from a heightened awareness of language, brought about largely with the aid of the ear, foster perceptive reading and eloquent writing.

In a vigorous defense of the value of memorizing texts, Thomas Newkirk suggests that learning "by heart" accomplishes all that reading aloud does, and more. Committing texts to memory, so they can readily be called up and voiced, acknowledges their value—their ideas and style and beauty. In memorizing a text, Newkirk suggests, we pledge "allegiance" to it in "an act of loyalty and deep respect" (*Slow Reading* 76). That respect extends to the artistry of the memorized texts, an artistry reflected in their styles and voices, which benefit from being heard.

We can ask yet another variation of our original question. Instead of "What does the text *say*?" we can ask, "What does the text *do*?"

This question invites a consideration of technique. It encourages us to examine not only the effects a text produces, but also the manner in which the writer creates those effects. Asking what a text *does* before asking what it *means* gives us time to consider its language and form, to make observations and connections among its words and images, its syntax and structure, even the purpose and effects of its punctuation.

You must have noticed, for example, how William Carlos Williams omits punctuation in some of the poems quoted earlier, how he uses punctuation selectively. You observed, too, I suspect, how he employs capitalization differently across those poems—sometimes capitalizing words at the beginning of lines, sometimes not, and exhibiting a similar kind of inconsistency with capitalization at the beginning of sentences. We can't get to the significance of these details without first noticing them. Asking what a text "does" nudges us toward such noticing. And following that noticing comes thinking about we have observed.

Asking what a text *does* acknowledges its expressive power, its ability to arouse feeling as well as provoke thinking. This question encourages attention to how texts move us as well as instruct us; it directs us to their emotional resonance as well as their cognitive significance. In reading the New Testament parable of the prodigal son, for example, we can slow things down to highlight dramatic moments in which characters' feelings are paramount. We can attend to the text through both intellectual comprehension and emotional apprehension, responding to the powerful feelings the textual details generate.

Our original dominant question and its two variants enable us to engage texts on many levels—the personal and private as well as the impersonal and public, affectively and subjectively, as well as rationally and analytically. The three aspects—what texts *mean*, what texts *say*, and what texts *do*—invite us to inspect their words scrupulously and then to respond to them, contextualize them, and experience their manifold pleasures.

Reading with Questions

We can read with questions about a writer's choices of diction and syntax, image and example, sound and sense, structure and conceptual implications. We can consider questions about a work's effects, its assumptions and values, its genre and form, its nature and purpose. The questions that emerge as we read should arise organically from experiencing a text's claims and evidence, its narrative, its voice and tone and texture, its exposition, argument, and other features.

At their best, our questions about texts prompt us to think about them more thoroughly and more expansively. Our questions encourage analysis and appreciation, and they invite us to explore the ways texts stimulate our feelings and our thoughts about them. The three types of questions we have considered thus far are suggestive rather than exhaustive. They help us approach literary works in a spirit of inquiry and exploration, joyously, without seeking a single, absolute, final, and definitive interpretive answer to their meaning.

All interpretations of a text, however, are not equally valid, equally persuasive, or equally useful. Some interpretations are more persuasive than others; some are more interesting, more convincing, more elegant. Employing a range of questions about texts invites us to consider their extrainterpretive dimensions—our feelings and noncognitive responses, which, counterintuitively, may well lead us to a more richly nuanced interpretation. Broadening the range of questions we ask about texts not only helps us see more in them, but also inspires a more richly rewarding reading experience.

Before returning to our original question—"What does the text mean?"—we can consider two additional variations: "What does the text *show*?" (or "What does the text *reveal (and conceal)*?" And "What does the text *suggest*?" Each of these questions leads us to read texts in still other ways, though ultimately, of course, taking us back to considerations of textual meaning. Essentially, then, in exploring these four variations of our text-as-meaning question—*saying* and *doing*, *showing* and *suggesting*—we expand the meaning of a text's "meaning."

So, then, what does the text "show" and what does it avoid showing, even refuse to show? How much and what does it reveal, and what might it conceal? Asking these related questions invites us to analyze a text's implications—what it does not state outright, what it does not say directly. Considering what a text "shows" can highlight a text's visual qualities, its images, its scenes, its way of describing. The classic advice given writers—"Show, don't tell"—directs readers to see what the text shows rather than what it says, what it depicts rather than what it explains. Many texts both show and tell. What they tell may be in conflict with what they show. Critics adept at deconstructive readings provide skillful examples of how texts are conflicted, at odds with themselves, how they undermine and sabotage themselves through gaps and contradictions, through forms of showing something other than what they tell.

More traditional critics, formalist critics, for example, look carefully to see what texts show and acknowledge what they don't, whether or not what those texts reveal conflicts with what they tell—if they tell anything overtly at all.

Literary works, by their nature, suggest rather than explain; they imply rather than state their claims boldly and directly. This broad generalization, however, does not mean that works of literature do not include direct statements. Depending on when they were written and by whom, literary works may contain large amounts of direct telling and lesser amounts of suggestion and implication, as in omniscient narration, for example. But whatever the proportion of a work's showing to telling, there is always something for readers to interpret. Thus we ask the question "What does the text suggest?" as a way to approach literary interpretation, as a way to begin thinking about a text's implications. What a text implies is often of great interest to us. And our work of ferreting out a text's implications tests our analytical powers. In considering what a text suggests, we gain practice in making sense of texts. And the primary way we do that is by looking closely at a text's language and details.

Let's listen to the opening of a perennially popular novel: Jane Austen's *Pride and Prejudice*. What do we notice about the beginning: to what does Austen direct our attention? What does Austen *say* and *do*, *show* and *suggest*, in this famous opening?

It is a truth universally acknowledged, that a single man in possession of a good fortune must be in want of a wife.

However little known the feelings or views of such a man may be on his first entering a neighborhood, this truth is so well fixed in the minds of the surrounding families, that he is considered as the rightful property of some one or other of their daughters.

"My dear Mr. Bennet," said his lady to him one day, "have you heard that Netherfield Park is let at last?"

Mr. Bennet replied that he had not.

"But it is," returned she; "for Mrs. Long has just been here, and she told me all about it."

Mr. Bennet made no answer.

"Do not you want to know who has taken it?" cried his wife impatiently.

"You want to tell me, and I have no objection to hearing it."

This was invitation enough.

"Why, my dear, you must know, Mrs. Long says that Netherfield is taken by a young man of large fortune from the north of England; that he came down on Monday in a chaise and four to see the place, and was so much delighted with it that he agreed with Mr. Morris immediately; that he is to take possession before Michaelmas, and some of his servants are to be in the house by the end of next week."

"What is his name?"

"Bingley."

"Is he married or single?"

"Oh! Single, my dear, to be sure! A single man of large fortune; four or five thousand a year. What a fine thing for our girls!"

"How so? How can it affect them?"

"My dear Mr. Bennet," replied his wife, "how can you be so tiresome! You must know that I am thinking of his marrying one of them."

What does this famous text *say*? What does it *do*? What does it *show*? And what does it *suggest*? We can answer each of these questions briefly before considering their implications in more detail.

In listening to what the text "says," we hear three voices—the voice of the narrator, which begins the novel, and which interpolates three brief comments between the voices of two characters, Mr. Bennet and Mrs. Bennet. What do we hear in each of these voices? What impression do we gain of Mr. and Mrs. Bennet by listening to their dialogue? What impression do we gain of the narrator through the novel's opening sentences and those three brief interpolated comments? What impression does the narrative voice convey about Mr. and Mrs. Bennet? These are the kinds of questions useful for listening to a text's voices.

In asking, next, what the text "does," we might say simply that it introduces us to two things: to the novel's primary subject—marriage and its connection with money and status—and to a pair of important characters, who we soon learn have five daughters in need of marital partners.

Viewing the text from the perspective of "showing," we might say that it shows us what's important in the world of the novel. It provides a quick look, too, at the novel's setting—in the country rather than the city, in rural England in the late eighteenth century, when Austen wrote the novel, though it wasn't published until 1813. Country estates are briefly mentioned and will become a central concern of the Bennet family as the novel progresses.

To consider what the text "suggests" is to engage in speculation about the importance of what it *says*, *does*, and *shows*. We can consider what this brief excerpt of Austen's novel suggests by asking questions about its language and selection of detail—about what the author chooses to tell us through the remarks of her narrator, and what she chooses to let us overhear in her characters' dialogue.

To gain access to what the text suggests, we need to ask a few questions about it. Is it a truth—that is, do we accept as fact what the opening sentence seems to assert: that a single man of means must be looking for a wife? Do we believe that this search for a wife is a phenomenon universally acknowledged, recognized around the world in other times and places, and not merely in the time and place of Austen's novel? Is it possible that Jane Austen's sentence means the opposite of what it purports to suggest: that single men of means more often than not are *not* in search of wives at all? How would we go about determining whether the sentence is ironic—whether what it says overtly and what it implies covertly are at odds, discrepant, and thus should not be taken at face value?

We can feel confident about the ironic tone of Austen's first sentence when we consider it in relation to the sentence that follows it. There we are told that knowledge of the eligible bachelor's feelings and views is of little if any importance. Clearly, however, the man's feelings and views should be a prime concern (especially a wealthy man in eighteenth-century England). That his feelings are unknown suggests they are of no consequence to the families, all intent on marrying off one of their daughters to the gentleman. This, of course, is ironic, the opposite of what might be expected in such a situation. And then there is the irony concerning ownership: that a man of wealth would be considered the rightful property of some marriageable daughter. A further irony is that marriageable eligibility is determined by wealth alone, with character, intelligence, wisdom, virtue, and other admirable and presumably desirable qualities in a spouse, ignored entirely. In this world, marriage matters; money matters; status and rank matter. Personal feelings do not matter—at least to Mrs. Bennet.

Portraying characters whose view of marriage is so mercenary, Austen distances herself from them and from their avaricious values. She does this through the comments of her narrator. This ironic distance is enforced when the author describes the misconceptions of her characters about single men, along with their reversal of the common notion that a wife is a man's property.

For these and other reasons, as the chapter and the novel develop, Austen displays an ironic tone that she uses to satirize Mrs. Bennet, as well as a number of other characters who make their appearance later. In these opening lines of her novel, and throughout its brief opening chapter, Austen teaches us how to read *Pride and Prejudice*—how to consider what it says and does, what it shows and suggests, and, ultimately, what it comes to mean for readers.

From "What" to "How"

Implicit in much of what I have said with respect to the sample texts previously discussed is the notion of literary artistry, which becomes explicit in what ensues here. We need to adjust our original question one last time—changing "what" to "how": from "*What* does the text mean?" to "*How* does the text mean?" What are the implications of this change? What does this variation do, say, and suggest? How does this new "how" question help readers discover the meaning(s) of a text?

In a way, our four variants of the ur-question, along with our attention to textual meaning through *saying* and *doing, showing* and *suggesting*—our considerations of textual implication—have led us to *how* a text means what it does. Our "how" question directs us toward technique, toward craft and art, toward the many and varied ways writers say, show, suggest, and do things with words as they create literature.

Let's have a look, first, at a brief poem by Langston Hughes, one of his best-known and most frequently anthologized pieces. (Many readers will recognize its second line as the title of a play by Lorraine Hansberry, *A Raisin in the Sun*, which was made into a popular film.)

Langston Hughes

DREAM DEFERRED [HARLEM 2]

What happens to a dream deferred?

Does it dry up like a raisin in the sun?
Or fester like a sore—
And then run?

Does it stink like rotten meat?
Or crust and sugar over—
Like a syrupy sweet?

Maybe it just sags
like a heavy load.

Or does it explode?

In this celebrated poem, Hughes relies on simile and metaphor to suggest a range of meanings. A pair of similes occupy each of the three-line stanzas, and a single simile stanza four. Hughes concludes by shifting from simile to metaphor, which he presents in a separate stanza, as the poem's conclusion. The stanzas become progressively shorter and increasingly emphatic. The final line, which employs metaphor, differs from the other poetic comparisons that precede it, redirecting the poem's energy and discharging its cumulative, pent-up force.

Hughes builds his poem from a fundamental question: "What happens to a dream deferred?" The rest of the poem consists of answers in the form of questions, with the penultimate answer a statement (though it works much like a question with the hypothetical "Maybe"). Hughes invites us to think about the implications of each of his questioning answers.

Our understanding of the poem hinges on how we interpret its opening question. What is being asked about a deferred dream? What type of "dream" is the poet inviting us to think about? What kind of dream is at stake? And once we move to a metaphorical or symbolic reading, we begin to consider what the deferral of those dreams might do to an individual or a group of people, whatever their race or skin color, but certainly including the dream of racial equality for African Americans, prominent among the deferred dreams that loom large for them.

Questions beget questions, each comparison inviting interpretive consideration, each simile suggesting yet another way a dream's deferral leads to its destruction. The various similes suggest different ways an unrealized dream results in undesirable, even destructive consequences. The final comparison is like the earlier ones, yet also differs from them. This concluding metaphor occupies a single line only, making it more emphatic; *italics* provide additional emphasis. And then there's that final word: *explode*. You don't get more conclusive—or explosive—than that.

Slowing things down this way allows us time to process what the poem says and suggests, what it shows and does. It gives us a chance first to notice and then to connect the kinds of details noticed—and how. Only then, after we've have had a chance to make observations and establish relationships among them, might we begin making inferences and drawing provisional interpretations about the poem.

And whether different readers focus on the unrealized nature of individual dreams or the deferral of social dreams of groups of people, all readers need to consider the implications of the poem's final line with its metaphor of explosion. What kind(s) of explosion, we might ask? And with what consequences?

If "Dream Deferred [Harlem 2]" is constructed almost exclusively of questions, the following poem, "The Art of Failing," includes only assertions. The poem is inspired by Elizabeth Bishop's "One Art," a poem about "the art of losing," whose rhyme on "master" and "disaster" I borrow and repurpose.

Robert DiYanni

THE ART OF FAILING

The art of failing isn't hard to master.
Just draft your project with the aim to fail.
Then fail better and fail faster. Skirt disaster.

Success is fine, but no match for failing well.
Fail better, fail faster, and be smart.
The art of failing isn't hard to master.

So Samuel Beckett says about his art.
Perfection eludes us at every turn.
So fail better and smarter to forestall disaster.

You won't get anything right from the start.
Don't try. Forgive yourself; make a mess.
Avoid duress. Fail smarter to prevent disaster.

Failure, not success, is what you're after.
That's where the surprises lurk—the discoveries.
The art of failing isn't hard to master.

Court failure. Don't fear its painful pleasure.
Follow missteps—embrace them, take their measure.
The art of failing you can learn to master.
Fail better, smarter, faster. Avert disaster.

Besides its use of the declarative mode, one of the first things we notice about "The Art of Failing" is its two repeating lines, the first and third of the poem (though these lines vary slightly in their repetitions as the poem progresses). Along with this syntactic repetition we also hear the echo of rhyme repeating throughout the poem, with the first and third lines of each three-line stanza rhyming with each other until the final stanza. The second line of each stanza rhymes with every other second line, including the second line of the slightly longer last stanza.

In short, we notice the poem's form, that of the villanelle, a nineteen-line poem with the opening line repeating in alternate stanzas as the last line of stanzas 2, 4, and 6 (though in this final stanza it is the third line of four). A villanelle's third line repeats in similar fashion, alternating among the odd-numbered stanzas before closing the poem off in its concluding line in slightly varied form.

The tone of "The Art of Failing" is far less urgent than that of Hughes's "Dream Deferred [Harlem 2]." Its statements explain and advise. They make assertions about how failing is an art that can be learned, and that learning the art of failure isn't all that difficult. (Early in the poem, however, we might wonder whether the speaker is being serious.) The reader is advised to embrace failure, to "court" it, even. The poem's advice runs counter to normal expectations and to conventional wisdom. Most people try to avoid failure, which can be costly both financially and emotionally, although there are those who believe that we can all learn from failure.

"The Art of Failing," however, takes this valuing of failure to another level. It's not just that we can learn from failure, the poem suggests; it's more that we should seek multiple opportunities and ways to fail. Through frequent practice with failure we can learn to fail "better" and "smarter." That seems to be the speaker's recommendation; it's what the poem appears to advise.

"The Art of Failing" is ironic in reversing our expectations about failure. It's also ironic in suggesting that through embracing failure we can "forestall disaster," which normally we would do by avoiding failure at all costs. Whether it's also, simultaneously, ironic about its recommendation to fail often is left for the reader to decide. Some readers, for example, might agree that failure is valuable for the reasons the poem suggests. But they might resist the impulse to look for ways to fail.

Unlike Hughes's poem, which works, largely, through a series of comparisons—both similes and metaphors—"The Art of Failing" avoids them. It offers, instead, a series of admonitions: do this, don't do that; this is what you should seek; this is what you should value.

We also notice how the poem uses rhyme and repetition, how its informal tone plays up the value of failure in our lives. Exact rhymes and slant, or approximate, rhymes are abundant: "faster" and "disaster"; "smart," "art," and "start"; "won't" and "don't"; "mess," "duress," and "success"; "after," "master," and "disaster"; "pleasure" and "measure," "skirt" and "avert." Finally, you likely noticed as well the heavy use of alliteration: "failing," "fail," "faster"; "fine," "failing," "fail," "fail," failing"; "fail," "forestall"; "forgive," "fail"; "failure," "failing"; "failure," "follow," "failing," "fail," "faster."

"The Art of Failing" takes pleasure in playing with all those rhymes and repetitions. While observing the "rules" of the villanelle, the poem entertains readers while simultaneously instructing them. Slowing down to enjoy the poem's verbal play increases our pleasure in reading it. The poem's rhymes and repeating sounds, words, and lines help us remember what it advises. That, we might surmise, is the poet's intention. What any reader, ultimately, makes of it, though, remains entirely the decision of that reader. And one thing we know for certain is that different readers will make different sense of this or any poem.

Conclusion

Postponing the question about a text's meaning through variations on it can broaden and deepen understanding of textual meaning(s). Coming at texts from different questioning directions allows for a wider range of interpretive possibilities than does insisting upon a text's meaning before we have a chance to hear what it says, notice what it does, see what it shows, and consider what it suggests. Doing those things enables us to analyze how it creates meaning. In addition, we question a text's ways of saying and doing, showing and suggesting—analyzing how a text means what it does—in relation to its genre and rhetorical potentialities. And we also consider a text in relation to the contexts of its author's life and work, as well as the context of its milieu.

Using these questions and their affiliated approaches to textual analysis rewards any reader's efforts. Postponing the question of meaning to consider what a text says and does, shows and suggests—and how—sharpens critical insight while deepening interpretive understanding. Delaying the meaning question in these ways leads to a fuller, richer, and more pleasurable encounter with texts, especially with works of literature.

If we accept this approach to reading literature and other serious works, why might we wish to engage with them? What's the payoff? we might ask. One answer among others proposed in the following chapters is that this deliberative way of reading aids in the search for truths that literature and other serious writing makes possible. Our primary reasons for reading are to acquire knowledge, deepen understanding, experience pleasure, and even, as we attain these ambitious goals, attain wisdom we might live by. Isn't that what we want from our reading, especially from our reading of literature?

two Reading for the Truth

EXPERIENCING, INTERPRETING, AND EVALUATING WHAT AND HOW WE READ

What we get from every text is precisely
balanced by what we give.
—ROBERT SCHOLES

What does it mean to ask what truth(s) a text tells? Is that what we should be reading literary works and other texts for? What does it mean to seek the truth(s) literary works convey and embody? Perhaps we should remember that it is the *search* for truth(s) as much as the *discovery* of truth(s) that matters—as Socrates, Leonardo, and Montaigne, among others, have reminded us over the centuries.

Is There a Truth about the Text?

To answer this question, I must be, initially at least, equivocal. Thus "yes" and "no." Yes, there is a Truth (with a capital *T*) about the text. But it is a Truth that we will never entirely encompass or fully understand. "Truth" with a capital *T* cannot be completely recoverable. So "yes," there is a Truth, and "no," we can't completely know what that Truth is.

And again: "Yes," there is a truth (with a lowercase *t*), if we mean one of any number of truths, some of which, having been recognized, we may agree on. But "no," if we insist that this "truth" is singular, definitive, absolute. There are multiple truths because texts are read and interpreted by readers in different ways.

Is there a "truth" about the text? "Yes," and "no." "Yes," but "no."

This constitutes my initial quick circuit of the question. And although my equivocal answer makes, I would submit, some sense, it is not adequate to our needs. And so it is necessary to make another pass at it.

Is there a Truth contained in the text? What do we mean by the "truth" of a text? For the sake of argument, let us say that the truth of a text is its accuracy and precision—the extent to which it reflects life as we experience it, knowledge as we understand it, the external world as we recognize it, wisdom as we know it. This is the truth of correspondence.

Along with this truthful textual correspondence, however, we recognize the truth of coherence—the unity and internal harmony of the text, its self-consistency, its integrity. Whether we think of the text as an organic growth or as a mechanical (re)production, a text's coherence resides in the way its parts relate to one another efficaciously. Part and whole, form and function, microcosm and macrocosm, the text lives as an entity complete within itself; yet it also exists simultaneously in relationship to something outside itself. Literature, like language generally, describes and explains something "out there"; language and literature reflect external reality while simultaneously interpreting it, when not (re)inventing it.

But these are familiar, even comforting notions. Let's circle back once more to consider whose truth the text reflects and represents, what kinds of truth it endorses and enforces. Once more, here, I take "truth" to indicate meaning, significance, what we understand a text to say and suggest, illustrate and demonstrate, reveal and, perhaps, conceal. We need to ask what the text means and says to whom. To all readers, or only to some readers? To experienced readers only or to the less experienced as well? To teachers, but not yet to students still developing as competent readers?

Which of the multiple truths are we talking about, anyway: the author's truth; the reader's truth; the teacher's truth; the student's truth? All these different truths for the various authors, readers, teachers, and students? Yet surely there must also somehow be some core or kernel of truth these diverse groups can agree on, can accept as a central textual truth. Should there be or could there be such a truth of the text?

Let's begin with the author's truth. An author's text has a truth to tell even if, as Emily Dickinson advises, she should "tell it slant," and that truth comes as a "superb surprise" (494). Moreover, the truth of the text is there even if, as Nathaniel Hawthorne often suggests, it comes veiled—as Robert Frost playfully and Herman Melville tragically indicate. We remember most, perhaps, what John Keats writes about the dynamic identity of beauty and truth in the famous ending to his "Ode on a Grecian Urn":

> "Beauty is truth, truth beauty,"—that is all
> Ye know on earth, and all ye need to know. (283)

Keats's relation of truth with beauty was anticipated by Shakespeare in a number of sonnets, notably sonnet 14: "truth and beauty shall together thrive"; and sonnet 54: "O, how much more doth beauty beauteous seem / By that sweet ornament which truth doth give!" A few centuries later Ralph Waldo Emerson added another term to the equation—"goodness"—equating each virtue with the others in a holy trinity discovered and celebrated not in churches and creeds but in the heart of nature. Here's how Emerson puts it in "Nature": "Truth, and beauty, and goodness, are but different faces of the same All" (19).

Indeed, the beauty of truth and the truth of beauty might be all we know and need to know, if, indeed, we could discover and really know truth through Dickinson's slant truth telling; through Hawthorne's veiled truths of the human heart; through Frost's truths about humans' relationship with the natural world; through Keats's truths about indolent autumn, full-throated nightingales, or "still unravished bride[s] of quietness and slow time" (282); through Emerson's truths of nature's divinity—to say nothing of Melville's Captain Ahab attempting to "strike through the mask" (967), seeking but not finding ever elusive Truth with a capital *T*.

Our quest for the truth of the text, then, is no simple matter. It doesn't begin and end in a single sweep of thought. Our way toward the truth of the text most often involves a return, a recursive circling back, a reentering of the text, always by way of its language, its structure, and its genre. And yet, additionally, our quest also goes by way of what we bring to it by virtue of our accumulated knowledge and our lived experience. The author's truth is neither singular, nor absolute, nor definitive. Even when the author explains a text's meaning—the truth of the tale—we do well, as D. H. Lawrence has warned us: "Never trust the artist. Trust the tale" (3). This advice, of course, has the effect of turning us back on ourselves to determine what the text's truths might be. The truth of the text, thus, is always the author's truth as determined by readers, a truth-seeking negotiation that never ends. Ultimately, then, authors' truths are readers' truths. There is no escaping this readerly reality and the concomitant responsibility it entails.

But what are these truths of readers? For me these are the living truths of the text, those truths that the text brings to life for us, those truths that connect, in some authentic and memorable way, with our lives. We read texts, as Robert Scholes notes, in the light of what we have lived (*Protocols* 10). To this I would add, on the flip side, that we live in the light of the texts we have read. The texts that matter to us become what we might call "life-texts," not merely texts that come to life for us in reading, but texts that enrich and complicate our lives. Such texts yield something of value for us because of what we bring to them and because of what we take from them. The truth of the text, thus, for readers, involves the ways we link the text with our lives, the ways we experience the intertextual web of literature, life, and language.

This approach to textual truth combines reader responsiveness to the text with responsibility to it. It is this dialectic between responsiveness and responsibility, textual submission and resistance, that motivates, enlivens, complicates, and completes the act of reading.

But what does it mean to be responsive to a text? And how do we exercise responsibility in our reading of it? Response and responsibility constitute the poles of a deliberative and fair critical reading, leading to interpretation grounded in careful observations, insightful connections, valid inferences, and thoughtfully considered values. A productive critical *reading* informs and is informed by critical *thinking* in reciprocal interplay. Critical reading and thinking capacities can benefit from a framework that includes making observations and connections, drawing inferences and interpretive conclusions, and considering a text's social, cultural, political, ethical, and other values.

To do this analytical work well, however, readers need to overcome an initial resistance to a text, the impulse to contradict, counter, or otherwise challenge it. Effective critical readers remain open to what a text offers. They are patient. The performance artist/actor Matthew Goulish provides one approach to this kind of textual receptiveness. In his essay "Criticism" from *39 Microlectures*, Goulish suggests that when we encounter any work of art, including imaginative works of all kinds (and by extension any verbal text), we should look for "moments of exhilaration." These special moments of textual encounter may be provoked by something exciting, engaging, or striking in a text, something that stirs our feelings, spurs our thinking, sparks our imagination.

Here is how Goulish puts it:

> We may then look to each work of art not for its faults and shortcomings, but for its moments of exhilaration, in an effort to bring our own imperfections into sympathetic vibration with these moments, and thus effect a creative change in ourselves. These moments will, of course, be somewhat subjective, so that if we don't find one immediately, we will out of respect look again. . . . In this way we will treat the work of art, in the words of South African composer Kevin Volans, not as an object in this world but as a window into another world. If we can articulate one window's particular exhilaration, we may open a way to inspire a change in ourselves, so that we may value and work from these recognitions. (45)

This way of engaging with a text requires withholding the tendency to find something wrong with it, something to criticize. Instead, it emphasizes something that's right with the work, something exhilarating, anything at all that might prove useful—a vivid detail we admire, a discernible pattern that aids our understanding, an assertion that provokes our thinking, a question we begin answering for ourselves. Through these "moments of exhilaration" we establish a personal relationship with the text in ways that can lead to "a creative change in ourselves." The kinds of "recognitions" that arise from openness to a text or work are recognitions as much about us as about what we read.

Rebecca Solnit argues that criticism is less about nailing things down than about investigating, exploring, and celebrating them. Taking Virginia Woolf as her model and mentor, Solnit describes a kind of "counter-criticism" that Woolf's essays exemplify in their avoidance of reading things as finished, certain, stable, and secure. Solnit argues for a criticism that leaves matters open, that avoids any attempt to constrict, contain, or classify, but that instead "respects the essential mystery of a work of art" (*Men Explain* 101), while recognizing its beauty and its pleasures.

In reading responsibly, we assume that a text possesses meaning. We give it, from this perspective, the benefit of the doubt. Our goal as responsible readers is to understand what a text means and to accurately represent that meaning in verbal or written form. In reading responsibly, we try faithfully to follow an author's line of reasoning and to understand his or her perspective even when—especially when—the author's ideas, concepts, values, and perspectives differ from or conflict with our own.

Once readers have learned to read responsibly by attending carefully to texts, they can begin to assume authority over their reading, exercising power by talking back to those texts. They can balance giving texts a fair hearing with offering a judgment and critique earned through thoughtful, reflective, analytical reading.

In "The American Scholar," Ralph Waldo Emerson writes, "There is then creative reading as well as creative writing" (*Essays* 59). For Emerson, reading is active and purposeful; it bears fruit in original thinking and writing. "First we read," he notes in his journal; "then we write" (*Journals* 8:320). The sequence is natural, even inevitable. Out of our reading, indeed in the process of reading, we wrestle with words and ideas; moreover, we generate ideas and develop our thinking. We reflect and make meaning. In "History," Emerson urges the student to "read history actively and not passively; to esteem his own life the text and books the commentary" (*Essays* 239).

The reciprocity between reading and thinking, along with the dynamic interchange between responsible and responsive reading, reflects the relationship between reading and living. It involves the consistent and extensive making of connections, both within texts and among and beyond them. As Maryanne Wolf notes in *Reader, Come Home*, "Deep reading is always about *connection*: connecting what we know to what we read, what we read to what we feel, what we feel to what we think, and how we think to how we live out our lives in a connected world" (163).

Reflective reading enriches and guides our lives, and, conversely, our lives enable and enhance our reading. Reading and living animate and invigorate one another in reciprocal interplay. The books we read speak to one another and affect each other, combining in various ways in our minds and hearts. They form an intertextual web that includes not only their relationships among themselves, but also their relationships with us, who engage in lifelong conversations with them. Henry David Thoreau suggests as much when he writes, "What I began by reading, I must finish by acting" (*Journal*, February 19, 1841)—even when "acting" winds up requiring additional reading.

The texts we read thoughtfully become part of our consciousness, part of who we are. This is true whether we are reading literary works or works of criticism. We become what we critically read, and as we continue to evolve as individuals, so do the books and mentors that have become part of us. We never finish with them, nor they with us. This is one of the wondrous pleasures and mysterious challenges of reading, especially of reading literature.

In a series of books about literary analysis and interpretation—*Semiotics and Interpretation* (1982), *Textual Power* (1985), and *Protocols of Reading* (1989), Robert Scholes grounds reader responsiveness and responsibility (my terms, not his) in genre and history, in language and in linguistic and cultural codes, by which and through which we make sense of texts and make sense of our lives. Genre and history, language and culture, matter in our encounters with texts, including the contextual circumstances that affect their production and reception. Scholes asks the same questions of all texts: What needs to be considered to understand the text? What were the conditions of the text's production? When, why, and how was it written? Who wrote it, under what circumstances, and for what purposes?

Sometimes we can answer these questions, and sometimes we can't. Considering them leads Scholes to the codes operative in all texts. He analyzes the codes of language and culture that create and constrain their meaning—genre, language, historical context, and cultural situation. The challenge of getting at textual truths involves deciding which codes are more or less relevant and how they function in the text. Gaining confidence and developing competence in acquiring this kind of literary discernment takes time and patience and practice.

Reading, Interpretation, Criticism

Scholes's approach to literary analysis encompasses "reading" (mostly personal responses); "interpretation" (a more objective analysis of literary devices and effects); and "criticism" (an opportunity to exercise judgment and consider values—social, cultural, personal, ideological, aesthetic). *Reading*, the primary activity upon which the others are situated, and which follow from it, is largely unconscious, though dependent on knowledge of codes and genres. In reading we construct a world from words, filling in gaps, making inferences and temporal connections, and more. Scholes explains, in *Textual Power*, how *interpretation* is a more deliberate, intentional, conscious activity, which "depends upon the failures of reading" (22). Interpretation requires explanation beyond summary. It is the result "either [of] an excess of meaning in a text or of some deficiency of knowledge in the reader" (22). As readers, we redress these interpretive deficiencies through analyzing the text, perhaps seeking help from others or from research.

Criticism involves an evaluation of the extent to which a literary work achieves or doesn't achieve "the purely literary norms of its mode or genre" (23). A more important and consequential aspect of criticism, however, involves a critique of the work's themes or a critique of the codes used to construct it. What we do as critical readers is encapsulated in this tidy formulation from *Textual Power*: "In *reading* we produce *text within text*; in *interpreting* we produce *text upon text*; and in *criticizing* we produce *text against text*" (24). In working through these three stages of textual encounter, we move from "a *submission* to textual authority in reading, through a *sharing* of textual power in interpretation, toward an *assertion* of power through opposition in criticism" (39; Scholes's italics throughout).

In this three-tiered approach, reading does not permit an interpretive possibility. It is, instead, personal, subjective, even narcissistic—inevitably so. Reading solely in a subjective mode, readers get out of a text only what they find in it, which, to some extent, is always themselves. The subjectivity of "reading" is a necessary starting point. We can't avoid bringing our subjectivity to the texts we encounter. And so we acknowledge our textual subjectivity and then move beyond it.

And yet, if our reading is overly subjective—insufficiently attentive to the "other" standing in and behind the text—there will be no real interpretation and no fair criticism, whether social, moral, political, rhetorical, or aesthetic. The consequence of subjective projection is to turn others into mirrors of ourselves. We need others, for without them there can be no dialogue, no conversation, no dialectic—just narcissism, solipsism, and self-love. Reading begins with forms of subjectivity; we can't go anywhere without starting there. However, we must get beyond subjectivity to arrive at interpretation and evaluation.

Because readers live unique lives and have had varied reading experiences, they perceive different features of the same texts, and they perceive the same features differently. Scholes provides an example in *Protocols of Reading* by highlighting feminism's "framing the question of reading inside the question of gender" (92). He suggests, further, how feminism has shown us the folly of thinking of an ideal reader reading a text that is the same for all (92).

Experience, Interpretation, Evaluation

Like Scholes's approach to literature, mine also includes three stages: (1) *experience*, (2) *interpretation*, and (3) *evaluation*. My approach begins with a reader's immediate experience of reading literary works—a reader's subjective and personal impressions of stories and poems, plays and essays. When we read a work of literature, something happens to us. The work may provoke us to think; it may move us emotionally; it might encourage us to do research or to engage in some type of action. It might make us laugh or cry; it might frustrate us, confuse us, amaze us, amuse us, provoke or stun us. It might remind us of our own or another's experience.

Each of us makes our way through a literary work somewhat differently. As we negotiate the lines of a poem, the sentences and paragraphs of a story or novel, the dialogue and stage directions of a play, we comprehend the text of the work according to the extent of our past experience with literature, the range of our language and vocabulary, and our knowledge of the contexts of the works we read. We may find a particular poem, story, or play, or an aspect of it, sad or funny, moving or exciting—or we may not. And we may find its surface relatively easy or relatively difficult to comprehend.

In responding to literary works in these and other ways, we bring our personal and shared human experience to our reading. This type of response is subjective, emotional, impressionistic; our *experience* of literature is real and unavoidable, but it is not enough for an adequate appreciation of literature. It is necessary and inescapable, but certainly not sufficient for a deep understanding of literary works.

As we consider why we respond as we do, and why we find a literary work's language and structure, content and context difficult or not, we move beyond our personal experience and toward interpretation. We move from the affective to the cognitive—from *emotional apprehension* of literary works toward *intellectual comprehension* of them.

Interpretation is based on analysis. Our understanding of literary works, like our understanding of all sorts of things, results from our effort to analyze and interpret, to explain them to ourselves, to make sense of their implications. Our *interpretation* of works of literature provides an intellectual counterpart to our emotional *experience* of them. When we interpret literary works, we concern ourselves less with *how they affect us*, and more with *what they mean*. Interpretation, in short, aims at understanding.

How do we come to understand works of literature? How do we develop an ability to interpret literature with competence and with confidence? One way is to become familiar with its basic elements: plot, character, and setting in fiction, for example; imagery, syntax, and sound play in poetry; dialogue, stage directions, and character relationships in plays; voice, structure, style, and tone in essays—though these elements cross genres, as well.

Another way in to literary understanding is through the structure of analysis more generally. All literary interpretation is grounded in *observation*—in careful noticing of a work's details, including its language and structure (as we have just seen). We seek connections among details, looking for patterns, such as contrast and conflict, repetition and variation. Based on our *observations* and *connections*, we make *inferences*, or educated guesses and surmises about possible meanings. We test our inferences as we read a work, and we think critically as we reread it, and as we talk about it with others.

Based on our inferences and our reconsiderations (which derive from our observations and connections), we formulate *provisional interpretations* of a work. That is, we come to some kind of understanding about its meaning(s) and significance. These interpretations are "provisional" because we can change our minds about them; we can revise our understanding of literary works based on further reading, research, conversation, and thinking. They are also *partial* in two senses: in being limited to our individual perspective, and in being incomplete, as there is always more to see and say and think about with respect to a literary work.

This tripartite framework begins with the personal, with responding to literature; it continues with a more objective, analytical approach based on literary elements; and it concludes with a consideration of values embedded in and embodied by literary works. And so in addition to our personal and subjective responses to literary works (*experience*) and our analysis of them (*interpretation*), we also consider their values—social, cultural, political, moral, and more (*evaluation*). This third, valued-centered, way to approach literature is related to experience and interpretation, in part derives from them, and in part drives them. In evaluating a story, poem, play, or essay, we do, largely, two things: (1) we assess its literary quality; and (2) we consider the values it embodies, whether or not those values seem to be endorsed, questioned, or challenged.

An evaluation is essentially a judgment, an opinion about a work formulated as a conclusion. In thinking about the New Testament parable of the prodigal son, for example, we may agree or disagree with the father's forgiveness of his wayward son or with the elder brother's complaint that the father never killed a fatted calf for him, the good and loyal son. We may confirm or criticize the behavior of literary characters in this way. However we evaluate them, though, we invariably measure the work's values against our own.

In evaluating a literary work, we appraise it according to our own special combination of social, cultural, moral, ideological, and aesthetic values. Our social and cultural values derive from our lives as members of families, communities, and larger social entities. These values are linked with our moral values and our ethical norms—what we believe to be right and wrong, good and evil. Our ideological values are grounded in our political convictions and, perhaps, the economic realities of our lives. Our aesthetic values reflect what we consider to be beautiful or ugly, well or ill made. Over time, with experience in life and with education, our values often change.

This is the case as well with all works of literature we read. A story we once admired for what it reveals about human behavior, or one whose moral perspective we accepted, we may come to consider later as trivial or erroneous. On the other hand, we may find works we initially disliked to be, on subsequent reading, appealing and engaging. Individual and collective literary tastes and values change over time. Social values and aesthetic attitudes shift. Works of literature, like musical works and political ideas, go in and out of fashion both for us and for the larger society as well.

Aesthetic values are, perhaps, the most difficult to discuss and understand. Our aesthetic sense is affected by impressions and feelings, sensations and memories, which tend to be elusive. Our aesthetic responses are linked with our expectations, which are influenced by our prior experience with reading literature. They are further complicated by our tendency to react quickly, even decisively, with our likes and dislikes. Consider the aesthetic value of the parable of the prodigal son. Is the parable well-constructed? Is it a strong and effective narrative? Does it seem to be a good example of its genre?

Our understanding of a work's genre also affects our aesthetic evaluation of it. Our preference for one type of fiction or one type or poetry, for example, for one genre of drama or one kind of essay, complicates matters further. We may dislike ironic poems or non-chronological stories; we may not appreciate nonrealistic works of drama or fiction, and not enjoy essays unless they are constructed as arguments (or as narratives).

How we arrive at aesthetic evaluation is affected by the informed responses of others, who likely have had experiences with life and literature different from those that we have had. Eventually, through the experience of living and reading literature, we develop a form of literary tact—an ability to distinguish good writing from bad, successful works from unsuccessful ones; we develop a kind of balanced judgment informed by thoughtful reflection. There are no shortcuts to acquiring an aesthetic appreciation of literature. Moreover, we will find that others do not necessarily see and experience and value any particular work of literature as we do. They may find different kinds of truths and value in it.

We can apply this reading framework to a short piece of prose, a single paragraph by E. B. White about the 1969 landing on the moon and the moonwalk of Neil Armstrong and Buzz Aldrin. Here is White's piece with its sentences numbered for ease of reference. I've provided a title, though White didn't, as his piece appeared as a column under the heading "Notes and Comment."

[Moonwalk]

The moon, it turns out, is a great place for men. (2) One-sixth gravity must be a lot of fun, and when Armstrong and Aldrin went into their bouncy little dance, like two happy children, it was a moment not only of triumph but of gaiety. (3) The moon, on the other hand, is a poor place for flags. (4) Ours looked stiff and awkward, trying to float on the breeze that does not blow. (5) (There must be a lesson here somewhere.) (6) It is traditional, of course, for explorers to plant the flag, but it struck us, as we watched with awe and admiration and pride, that our two fellows were universal men, not national men, and should have been equipped accordingly. (7) Like every great river and every great sea, the moon belongs to none and belongs to all. (8) It still holds the key to madness, still controls the tides that lap on shores everywhere, still guards the lovers who kiss in every land under no banner but the sky. (9) What a pity that in our moment of triumph we did not forswear the familiar Iwo Jima scene and plant instead a device acceptable to all: a limp white handkerchief, perhaps, symbol of the common cold, which, like the moon, affects us all, unites us all.

—E. B. WHITE, "NOTES AND COMMENT,"
NEW YORKER, JULY 26, 1969

Before considering what White's paragraph "means," what central idea White is suggesting about the moon landing, let's slow the process down. We'll consider first our experience of reading White's piece, and then turn to what we might notice about it. After a few observations, we'll proceed through the remainder of the framework, noting connections and inferences before providing some provisional interpretive thoughts along with a consideration of the paragraph's embedded values.

Experience

What is our experience reading White's paragraph? To what extent are we carried along with his portrayal of the moon landing, perhaps amused by how he characterizes it, perhaps surprised at certain details and images he includes in his description? Do we find the moonwalk paragraph interesting, engaging, entertaining? Does it provoke us to think? Do any particular details or assertions confuse us, amuse us, resonate strongly for us—either positively or negatively? How might we characterize our experience of reading White's mini-essay? These are the sorts of considerations our "experience" of a text highlights.

Observations

The single paragraph begins with a brief sentence and ends with a much longer one. White's sentences vary quite a bit in length, with three short sentences interspersed among half a dozen longer ones. White varies the length of his sentences to avoid monotony and enhance the paragraph's fluency.

The first sentence does two things: it makes an assertion and it creates surprise. Who would have thought (the surprise) that the moon (of all places) is "a great place for men"? Reading this sentence attentively, we wonder why White says what he does. We ask ourselves, "How" is the moon great for men? White's second sentence answers that question by positing two explanations: first, it is a place of triumph; second, it is a place of "gaiety," with White describing the two astronauts, Neil Armstrong and Buzz Aldrin, as "happy children" doing a "bouncy little dance."

These first two sentences are closely linked. The second provides specification for the first; it answers the question raised by the first, and suggests how the moon is "a great place for men." White compares the bouncy way men move on the moon (owing to its significantly lower gravity than earth's) to a "dance," illustrating their "gaiety."

White's opening differs in emphasis from what most other commentators highlighted at the time, focusing, mainly, on the astronauts' walk on the moon as "one small step for (a) man" and "one giant leap for mankind" (Armstrong's own famous formulation). Triumphant it certainly was, though White chooses to emphasize something other than that triumph, something, paradoxically, both humbler and more ambitious.

Our next move is to continue delaying the rush to interpretation by considering what connections among our observations might be made. What patterns or relationships among details can be established?

Connections

In terms of connections, we see (and hear) a shift—a change of tone as the paragraph proceeds. In sentences 3, 4, and 5, White shifts from the men's apparently happy movement—their "bouncy little dance"—to the American flag they planted on the moon's surface. The flag's stiffness, he suggests, is an indication of its awkwardness, its being out of place. The moon's atmosphere lacks the breezy force to make the flag wave in celebration of the Americans' triumphant walk on its surface. The fifth sentence's parenthesis injects a note of humor into its fundamental seriousness. The "lesson" White alludes to here he will develop in successive sentences.

These sentences shift from the celebratory tone of the paragraph's first two sentences to something graver. White's contrast between the active men and the static flag convey this shift in tone. And we might take up White's invitation to consider the lesson implied by the paragraph's first five sentences—particularly by sentences 3 and 4. We also note repeated words and details that are related. The word "flag," for example, is repeated later in the plural "flags" and echoed still later in the word "banner." The word "plant" is used twice—to plant the flag, which the astronauts did, and, as White whimsically but meaningfully suggests later, planting a handkerchief on the moon instead.

Other connections include references to nature—to river, sea, and sky, as well as to the moon. Considering the implications of these connections and repetitions leads us to meaning, initially through the inferences about those repeated terms and the references to the natural world.

Inferences

Perhaps the most challenging and important readerly move is the leap to inference. Based on the observations made and the connections established among them, what inferences might be drawn from the text? What initial thinking directions might emerge?

Making inferences leads us back to the text—for yet another look at (and listen to) its language and structure. Making inferences forces scrupulous textual observation; it prompts yet another pass at the text to consider it yet again, ideally reading it aloud to hear what it suggests, how and what its rhythms contribute to its meaning.

The process I am describing here is iterative and recursive. I don't want to suggest that it's simply linear, stepwise: first observations, then connections followed by inferences, and then on to the next and perhaps final stage of interpreting for meaning. Not at all. I am claiming, instead, that, although we begin with observations and connections, we need to circle back to those steps of noticing and relating details even after we have made a number of inferences. Our inferences, thus, prompt a return to the text for additional observing and connecting—and then on then on to additional inferences.

But let's return to White's prose piece. White builds out sentence 6, which is longer and more complex than the five sentences that precede it. He develops a contrast there between admiration and national pride for the astronauts' achievement and a more expansive sense of awe for their accomplishment, beyond patriotic fervor. He sees the moon landing as more than an American triumph. The moon, as White notes, "belongs to all," while, paradoxically, belonging to no one at all.

Provisional Interpretation

What provisional conclusions might we draw from White's paragraph? Foremost, that it's not just the moon that belongs to everyone and no one, but nature more generally. This paradox is true as well for "every great river and every great sea." White further develops his universalizing idea in sentence 8, which relies on familiar associations of the moon with madness and love, while simultaneously recognizing the moon's physical influence on watery tides "everywhere." In addition, White brings back the image of the flag in an implied comparison with the sky as a "banner" under which lovers kiss "in every land." We are thus given another kind of banner, a universal banner of blue, to contrast with the national banner of the stars and stripes.

White's paragraph about the moon landing acknowledges the amazing accomplishment it was. And yet White has something more for us to think about. His paragraph's concluding sentence conveys an important provocation. White's final sentence connects earlier descriptive details, enforcing and solidifying his idea that in emphasizing the moon landing as a human triumph, we miss a chance to see its larger human implications, in being an exciting yet imperfect achievement for humankind. In emphasizing it as a national American accomplishment, we miss an opportunity to see its universal significance. White invites us to consider the values associated with the moon landing and the ways we characterize its achievement.

Evaluation—Considering Values

White sees the moon landing as a tribute to human ingenuity as well as to American triumphalism, its space program a technological human marvel. And yet for all the triumphalism of the feat, White provokes other considerations beyond the values associated with either national or broader human achievement. White invites his readers to consider another way of thinking about the meaning of the moon landing.

He conveys these larger ideas with two related details at the end of his paragraph: his reference to the "familiar Iwo Jima scene" and his suggestion to replace the American flag with a white handkerchief, symbol of "the common cold." White refers to the iconic picture of American soldiers hoisting the flag after defeating the Japanese in World War II on the strategic Pacific island of Iwo Jima. He connects the moon landing to the important American victory only to suggest that there are other values at play and at stake in the moon landing, and that there are other ways to think about the significance of what was achieved that day in 1969, other more appropriate symbols by which that achievement might be represented, remembered, and revered.

We might also consider the historical context of the paragraph, first in relation to White's Iwo Jima allusion, and then in relation to the time in which it was written. We can consider how White's little piece was received at the time and how it compared with the many other pieces written about the moon landing, in newspapers and magazines and books. We can consider the cultural and political implications of White's moon landing paragraph for nationalism and internationalism, and how those ideas and their associated ideals have played out historically since 1969.

Literature and Argument

One additional way that literary works embody truths is through dialogue and debate. Literary characters disagree with one another, argue with one another, offer competing perspectives and counterviews. From the dialectic that drives Sophoclean tragedy, *Antigone* and *Oedipus the King* especially, to the repartee between characters in Shakespeare's comedies, to the witty exchanges we find in eighteenth- and nineteenth- century drama, argument is a literary staple. To recognize the various ways argument appears in literary works is not to suggest, however, that literature's purpose is to argue for any particular proposition or idea.

Literature offer us the opposite of what argument provides. Literary works don't assert anything; they don't make "claims," and literary characters or narrators who do make the kinds of claims and assertions characteristic of formal argument do so not in the name of the author or of the work, but only for themselves as characters at particular moments in the fictional worlds they inhabit. Iago, for example, speaks for himself, as does Othello, and not for Shakespeare.

The truths embodied in works of literature are diverse, varied, and multiple. What readers take from *Othello* varies from one reader to another, and for different readers at different times in their lives. Fiction writers and poets, as well as dramatists and essayists, employ argument in various ways. We consider next two examples: a poem in blank verse, "Mending Wall," by Robert Frost and a pair of speeches from *The Tragedy of Julius Caesar*. We will consider aspects of argument in each.

Robert Frost's "Mending Wall"—Contrasting Perspectives

As Tim Kendall points out in *The Art of Robert Frost*, "Mending Wall" can be considered in relation to debates about a range of topics, including "nationhood and internationalism, selfhood, neighborliness, the rituals of labor, the interactions between man and nature" (50)—and more. Those and other thematic provocations provide grist for the interpretive mill and the competing perspectives of argument. My interest here is how Frost engages us in the dialogue and debate between the poem's dueling speakers, the narrator and his walled-off neighbor. Because the poem is on the longish side, I've chunked it and followed with commentary on each section.

Here we go.

> Something there is that doesn't love a wall,
> That sends the frozen-ground-swell under it
> And spills the upper boulders in the sun,
> And makes gaps even two can pass abreast.
> The work of hunters is another thing:
> I have come after them and made repair
> Where they have left not one stone on a stone,
> But they would have the rabbit out of hiding,
> To please the yelping dogs. The gaps I mean,
> No one has seen them made or heard them made,
> But at spring mending-time we find them there.

COMMENTS

"Mending Wall" opens with a speaker suggesting that walls aren't universally loved or valued. But this notion is expressed in an unusual way, with the impersonal vagueness of "something" as subject of the statement and its odd syntax, which deviates from the more expected and normal pattern of "There is something." The deviation draws our attention, making the statement emphatic, elevating it above a flat ordinariness.

The opening lines invite us to consider the wall symbolically, since they suggest that even nature objects to it; it's not simply a matter of the speaker's dislike, although it is the speaker who seems to attribute to nature an intentionality, which, of course, is really his. He enlists nature in his dislike of stone walls by explaining how they fall into disrepair naturally, as a result of seasonal variations in temperature.

In these first lines, too, the speaker offers an additional reason for the wall's state of disrepair: hunters tear down parts of the wall when rabbit hunting. And though he has seen the hunters damaging the wall, he discovers nature's antiwall activities only after the fact. The end of this segment indicates that he is not alone in discovering the wall's disrepair, and repairs to the wall are done in spring.

> I let my neighbor know beyond the hill;
> And on a day we meet to walk the line
> And set the wall between us once again.
> We keep the wall between us as we go.
> To each the boulders that have fallen to each.
> And some are loaves and some so nearly balls
> We have to use a spell to make them balance:
> "Stay where you are until our backs are turned!"
> We wear our fingers rough with handling them.
> Oh, just another kind of outdoor game,
> One on a side. It comes to little more:

COMMENTS

We notice how the speaker himself initiates the ritualistic springtime wall repair and the manner in which the speaker and his neighbor go about their work. Instead of working together on one side of the wall, they "keep the wall between" them as they work. The image neatly illustrates one symbolic dimension of walls: they keep things and people apart. Ironically, however, in this instance, they also bring people together, though on opposite sides of their wall.

Frost, however, merely hints at this idea. He describes a scene that shows two men working together yet divided, apart yet connected, the wall they are repairing simultaneously separating and uniting them. The image and idea are both provocative and para-doxical, provocative because paradoxical: the men come to-gether in order to separate themselves; they join in rebuilding the wall that will continue to keep them apart. This double-edged image, moreover, is sustained through additional details; in the poem's diction of unity: *"We* have to use a spell"; till *"our* backs are turned"; *We* wear *our* fingers rough." This communal language, however, is counterpointed by words suggesting separateness: "To *each* the boulders that have fallen to *each"* and *"One* on a *side."*

One additional point is suggested in these lines: that the work is also play, a "game." This second paradox proposes that their work is at once serious and humorous, a matter of importance for each, but also "just another kind of outdoor game," a phrase the tone of which contributes to its sense of play. The poem continues:

> There where it is we do not need the wall:
> He is all pine and I am apple orchard.
> My apple trees will never get across
> And eat the cones under his pines, I tell him.
> He only says, "Good fences make good neighbors."
> Spring is the mischief in me, and I wonder
> If I could put a notion in his head:
> "Why do they make good neighbors? Isn't it
> Where there are cows? But here there are no cows.
> Before I build a wall I'd ask to know
> What I was walling in or walling out,
> And to whom I was like to give offense.

COMMENTS

The speaker signals the men's separation via the tree species that inhabit their adjoining properties, with his apple trees bearing leaves and fruit, differentiating them from the neighbor's pines with their cones and needles. The poet further distinguishes the two with the speaker's teasing remark that his apple trees won't in-trude on his neighbor's pines. Impervious to wit and lacking the speaker's sense of humor (and sense of superiority), the neighbor retorts with the famous saying "Good fences make good neighbors," a response that contrasts with the poem's and speaker's opening line: "Something there is that doesn't love a wall."

The poem's characters engage in a friendly competition, one with no apparent resolution. The dialectic in "Mending Wall" pits two contrasting ideas against each other, implying that both have merit, that each is, in some sense, right—that walls, paradoxically, have opposite consequences, "walling in" and "walling out," as the speaker notes, with both kinds of walling consequences of some use and value.

In this section, the speaker distances himself more and more from his neighbor. In addition to exercising his wit and playfulness, the speaker questions things: he wants to know *why* a particular wall exists, what it is supposed to do. In contrast, the neighbor lacks the speaker's impulse to wonder. He seems to neither need nor desire an explanation. He doesn't need to know why; he simply asserts what he has always believed, "Good fences make good neighbors," which he will repeat in the poem's final line, his repetition balancing the speaker's repeated dislike of walls. Here, then, is the last section with their echoing double refrain:

> Something there is that doesn't love a wall,
> That wants it down." I could say "Elves" to him,
> But it's not elves exactly, and I'd rather
> He said it for himself. I see him there,
> Bringing a stone grasped firmly by the top
> In each hand, like an old-stone savage armed.
> He moves in darkness as it seems to me,
> Not of woods only and the shade of trees.
> He will not go behind his father's saying,
> And he likes having thought of it so well
> He says again: "Good fences make good neighbors."

COMMENTS

In this final section of "Mending Wall," the speaker characterizes his neighbor as primitive, even dangerous. As the speaker describes the neighbor carrying two stones to place on the wall, he envisions him as a savage, precivilized, with stones as weapons. And so, once again, Frost provides us with a double perspective: the two men as neighborly, working together to rebuild the wall; the men as enemies, the neighbor a threat and danger to the speaker.

Perhaps more damning is the speaker's comment that the neighbor "moves in darkness," a darkness both literal (he moves in the shade of his pine trees) and figurative (the darkness is "[n]ot of woods only and the shade of trees"). The neighbor's darkness, the speaker implies, is a darkness of ignorance and superstition. He lacks an interest in logical explanation. There is, too, more than a touch of satire in the speaker's remark that the neighbor "likes having thought of [his statement] so well" that he repeats, "Good fences make good neighbors." This is ironic, of course, since the neighbor merely remembers this old saying, reciting what he's heard from his father, presumably without thinking about what it means or why he accepts what he is asserting.

Besides the poem's paradoxes and ironies, there is the question of what Frost the poet thinks of his speaker and the neighbor. He makes the speaker's point of view the prevailing one, yet he gives the last word to the neighbor. We are made to understand, too, that no matter what explanation the speaker might offer about why the wall is or isn't necessary, the neighbor will not budge from his stubborn insistence that "[g]ood fences make good neighbors."

And so where does that leave us readers? One place it leaves us is considering whether we understand and value what each speaker claims about the consequences of building walls—both intended and unintended consequences. Another is whether we embrace a form of dialectical reading in which we can appreciate two differing perspectives on the purpose and value of walls between neighbors, while retaining a preference for one view over the other.

We are also left to consider how Frost pulls off such a poetic stunt, making poetry out of common statements, turning matters of fact into art. Doing so, we might note the nimbleness and suppleness of Frost's writing. His language is clear and direct, rife with monosyllabic words. Except for the inverted syntax of the opening line, the poem's sentences are easy to follow, with the subject-verb-object construction the rule, and with some sentences one line each. Frost balances those short one-line sentences with longer ones, which ebb and flow across lines, sometimes stopping in a midline caesura, sometimes running over the end of one line into another. Through these line-crossing syntactic enjambments, Frost controls the rhythm and pacing of the poem, preventing it from becoming monotonous, which he also accomplishes by varying the regularity of its iambic pentameter pattern. In his inimitable way, Frost makes the complexity of art seem matter-of-fact, an easy straightforward way with words and ideas. What the Italians call *sprezzatura*.

Shakespeare and the Classical Oration

One of the strongest influences on the structure of an argument is the classical oration developed and used to brilliant effect by the orators of ancient Greece and Rome. The classical oration was meant to win the audience over to one side of a contentious debate. Its organizational structure highlights the ways that the speaker's claim and perspective differ from those of the opposition, and how and why the speaker's argument and claim are the stronger of the two.

Here is a brief outline of its main elements, along with a short explanation of each part's function.

1. *Exordium*. In this introductory section the speaker or writer introduces the subject or problem while attempting to secure the audience's good will. In *Words like Loaded Pistols*, Sam Leith notes that this is where "the strongest up-front ethos appeal will tend to come" (83).
2. *Narration*. Here, the speaker or writer puts the argument in context, presenting the facts of the situation, explaining what happened, when and where it occurred, who was involved, how and why. Reason and measured language are crucially important throughout this section.
3. *Partition*. Next, the speaker or writer divides up his subject, explaining the central issues, the key claim, and in what order the parts of the subject will be discussed.

Also included here is where we agree and disagree with
our opponents.

4. *Confirmation.* In this section, the speaker or writer
   provides detailed support through a careful selection of
   evidence and a logical approach to reasoning.

5. *Refutation.* The speaker or writer next identifies opposing arguments and refutes them by showing their
   weaknesses in claims and evidence. More use of logical
   reasoning, this time to rebut and refute rather than to
   confirm, as in the previous section.

6. *Peroration.* Finally, the speaker or writer summarizes
   the situation or case and attempts to move the audience
   to take action. This is the grand finale, in which pathos
   or appeals to emotion reach their height.

Instead of providing an example of an actual classical oration,
Greek or Roman, I offer one from drama, to complement our consideration of the argument in Frost's "Mending Wall." In the following example from *Julius Caesar,* the pair of speeches given by
Brutus and Mark Antony provide the bonus of being derived from,
while exemplifying, rhetorical practices of antiquity, which Shakespeare learned as part of his schooling.

In the first speech, Brutus, one of Caesar's murderers, addresses
Roman citizens to explain why Caesar's execution was necessary
and right. In the second speech, Mark Antony, friend to both
Brutus and Caesar, provides an alternative view of Caesar's death
at the hands of Brutus and his fellow conspirators.

We hear first from Brutus:

Romans, countrymen, and lovers! Hear me for my cause, and
be silent, that you may hear. Believe me for mine honor, and
have respect to mine honor, that you may believe. Censure
me in your wisdom, and awake your senses, that you may the
better judge. If there be any in this assembly, any dear friend
of Caesar's, to him I say that Brutus' love to Caesar was no
less than his. If then that friend demand why Brutus rose
against Caesar, this is my answer: Not that I lov'd Caesar less,

but that I lov'd Rome more. Had you rather Caesar were living, and die all slaves, than that Caesar were dead, to live all
freemen? As Caesar loved me, I weep for him; as he was fortunate, I rejoice at it; as he was valiant, I honor him; but, as
he was ambitious, I slew him. There is tears for his love; joy
for his fortune; honor for his valor; and death for his ambition. Who is here so base that would be a bondman? If any,
speak, for him have I offended. Who is here so rude that
would not be a Roman? If any, speak, for him have I offended.
Who is here so vile that will not love his country? If any, speak,
for him have I offended. I pause for a reply.

And now it's Mark Antony's turn:

Friends, Romans, countrymen, lend me your ears!
I come to bury Caesar, not to praise him.
The evil that men do lives after them,
The good is oft interred with their bones;
So let it be with Caesar. The noble Brutus
Hath told you Caesar was ambitious;
If it were so, it was a grievous fault,
And grievously hath Caesar answer'd it.
Here, under leave of Brutus and the rest,
(For Brutus is an honorable man,
So are they all, all honorable men),
Come I to speak in Caesar's funeral.
He was my friend, faithful and just to me;
But Brutus says he was ambitious,
And Brutus is an honorable man.
He hath brought many captives home to Rome,
Whose ransoms did the general coffers fill;
Did this in Caesar seem ambitious?
When that the poor have cried, Caesar hath wept;
Ambition should be made of sterner stuff:
Yet Brutus says he was ambitious,
And Brutus is an honorable man.
You all did see that on the Lupercal

I thrice presented him a kingly crown,
Which he did thrice refuse. Was this ambition?
Yet Brutus says he was ambitious,
And sure he is an honorable man.
I speak not to disprove what Brutus spoke,
But here I am to speak what I do know.
You all did love him once, not without cause;
What cause withholds you then to mourn for him?
O judgment! thou [art] fled to brutish beasts,
And men have lost their reason. Bear with me,
My heart is in the coffin there with Caesar,
And I must pause till it come back to me.

COMMENTS

In terms of the classical oration, as Gary Wills notes in *Rome and Rhetoric*, Brutus relies almost entirely on *partition*, or division, partitioning the key elements of Caesar's character and behavior: love, fortune, valor, and ambition. He arranges his list first with Caesar's three virtues, followed by the assertion that he was "ambitious," in Brutus's mind an irreparable vice for which he deserves death. Brutus's argument, however, omits evidence to support his claim about Caesar's ambition. Instead of providing evidence, Brutus simply repeats, in shorter measure, his first partition, culminating in "and death for his *ambition*."

In the next part of his spurious argument, Brutus challenges his audience by insisting, through a series of rhetorical questions, that any among them who disagree with his assessment and punishment are "*base*," "*rude*," or "*vile*." Steamrolling his listeners, Brutus sets up a false dichotomy between an imagined future in which his countrymen live in freedom or in slavery, according to whether Caesar is dead or alive. And this with no reasoning or evidence to support his claim. Finally, Brutus's speech, as Wills also notes, "is all about himself" (54). Though he uses his own name only twice in the speech, he uses forms of "me," "my," and "mine" eight times, and he uses "I" eleven times. Caesar's name is heard seven times.

Wills points out how Brutus appeals to his audience to trust him, to believe in him and what he has to say (57). Brutus implies that those who don't believe what he tells them about Caesar dishonor him, Brutus. He appeals to their sense of trust that he, Brutus, is an "honorable" man—a word that will reverberate in the speeches of both Brutus and Mark Anthony, though with significantly different implications.

Mark Antony's speech differs dramatically from Brutus's. Where Brutus appeals to fear, Antony appeals to feeling, relying on his hearers' sympathy for the slain Caesar. Where Brutus hammers home a single argument about Caesar's ambition and his own honor in justifying the murder of Caesar, Mark Antony uses a variety of persuasive strategies. In the process, he undermines Brutus and changes his listeners' minds.

In terms of classical oratory, Antony dispenses with narration, as Caesar's story is well known. Instead, like Brutus, he uses partition; but in the first major section of his speech he raises doubts about Caesar's ambition. Antony employs concession strategically to rebut Brutus's argument. He does so through repetition, referring to "ambition" seven times, casting doubt upon its applicability to Caesar. With each occurrence of the words "ambition" and "ambitious," their connection with Caesar becomes more tenuous.

Along with this repetition of "ambition," Antony repeats the word "honorable" over and over again, always with respect to Brutus: "for Brutus is an honorable man." This repetition of "honorable" accumulates irony, so that by the time Mark Antony is finished, his audience sees Brutus as anything but honorable; they see him, instead, as dishonorable for what he has done. Antony confirms Caesar's lack of ambition—the opposite of what Brutus claimed about Caesar, thereby refuting his argument that Caesar deserved death.

Antony uses questions skillfully throughout his speech and more subtly than does Brutus. Through his questions, Antony induces his listeners to reconsider their belief that Caesar was ambitious. Rather than insist that Brutus was wrong in that assertion, Antony invites his audience to reflect more fully and to consider examples of Caesar's behavior, after which he asks, essentially, "Was this ambitious?" "Does this seem ambitious to you?" Antony's questions, like Brutus's, are rhetorical; but they effectively sabotage Brutus's argument and undermine his defense of the conspirators' murder of Caesar.

It is Antony's peroration, however, that seals Brutus's fate. In this final section of his speech, Antony appeals directly and powerfully to the emotions of his audience. Antony elicits from his listeners the responses he desires (that he, Antony, is noble, a nobler man than Brutus), and draws them emotionally into the argument, arousing pity for Caesar along with anger at his killers. From there it's only a short step to action, for Antony's speech, unlike that of Brutus, is designed to encourage his listeners to *do* something, not simply to *believe* what he is saying. In a final and supremely effective dramatic move, Antony employs Caesar's dead and mutilated body as a prop, surrendering, as Wills suggests, "his orator's office to the corpse's own eloquence" (101). In a powerful display of visual rhetoric, Antony invites his listeners to engage in an act of imagination—to reexperience with him the moment of Caesar's death. As they do so, they are moved, finally, to take action against those responsible for his murder.

Perhaps the most effective overall rhetorical maneuvering Antony accomplishes in his speech is his disclaimer that he can speak effectively (and *affectively*). He pretends to lack oratorical skill, attributing that power to Brutus. He claims to speak directly and without artifice or ulterior motive (to "speak what I do know," he says). While producing the most powerful of persuasive effects, he denies both his intent and his ability to do so. In the process, Mark Antony displays, in ways Brutus decidedly does not, how rhetoric, skillfully and artfully wielded, creates its own reality.

This discussion of argument in literary works suggests that in seeking the truths that literature offers, we often find ourselves, *inevitably* find ourselves, engaging with competing perspectives. More often than not, our interpretation of literary works, as we noted from the start of this chapter, requires us to interpret and evaluate the uses of argument, overt and covert, they include. In the process, we determine for ourselves what counts as truth.

An Ethic of Reading

Texts are always good for something—lots of things, but not purely good, and not always good for the same things in the same ways for all readers. Nor for any particular reader all the time. I think we might claim that texts are good for *thinking with* and *thinking about*—for *thinking and feeling*, for educating the mind and the heart, for provoking thought and evoking feeling.

This is something of a Wordsworthian perspective, with feelings transformed into thoughts. In the Preface to his *Lyrical Ballads* Wordsworth writes that "our continual influxes of feeling are modified and directed by our thoughts, which are indeed the representatives of all our past feelings" (98). For Wordsworth, thought springs from feeling, influences and qualifies feeling. Feelings recollected and contemplated become thoughts. This idea is also akin to John Donne's notion of "felt thought"—of ideas animated by feeling, of feelings alive in thoughts. We might bring to bear here also T. S. Eliot's essay on the metaphysical poets, in which he suggests that Donne and other metaphysical poets felt their thought, that their thinking involved emotion as well as cognition. There is, in these poets, Eliot writes, "a direct sensuous apprehension of thought, or a recreation of thought into feeling" (246).

We don't have to believe everything an author believes. Nor do we have to accept what may feel philosophically or religiously alien to us—Hardy's fatalism, for example, Stevens's atheism, Tolstoy's theory of history, or Dante's vision of the afterlife. But in order to augment textual engagement and increase comprehension— interpretation and criticism—we may not have to believe, but we do need to know. And what we should know are the cultural codes, the conventions of genres, the meanings of words in historical context, and much more. This base of knowledge is essential for deeper literary appreciation and discernment.

We read, however, not only to comprehend, but also to connect texts with our lives and to incorporate them into ourselves. We read to make texts intelligible, to make meaning for our lives. If to some extent we are what we eat, we are very much also what we read. To make the most of these ways of reading, however, we need to acknowledge the importance of *experience, interpretation*, and *evaluation* for our reading practice. Without thinking about our experience of reading, we undervalue its subjective aspect. Without taking interpretive risks, we diminish our chance to develop understanding. Without considering a text's values, we neglect ways to test and strengthen—or modify and alter—our own beliefs and principles.

An ethic of reading also requires that we read as we would like to be read. We should read other texts with the same respect, the same deliberation, the same attention and care that we wish others might bring to our own writing. I'm paraphrasing and riffing a bit here on Thoreau in *Walden*: "Books must be read as deliberately and reservedly as they were written" (403). We could do worse than strive for this kind of attention to our reading. And we might imagine that all writers would hope to receive a similar degree of attention from their readers. It's perhaps the least we can do for those writers and the most we can hope for from ourselves as readers.

PART TWO Applications

THREE

Reading Nonfiction

ESSAYS, IDEAS, AND THE PLEASURES OF CONVERSATION

A good essay must have this permanent quality about it; it must draw its curtain round us, but it must be a curtain that shuts us in not out.
—VIRGINIA WOOLF

The Essay as a Literary Genre

Why read essays? Isn't there enough good and great literature—and entertaining literature—in the world's fiction, poetry, and drama? Why bother with essays?

Essays have long had an uncertain status as literature. Among the literary genres, the essay has frequently been considered the poor relation. A late arrival in the history of literature, the essay has been largely a practical tool. Used largely to inform and persuade rather than to entertain and move, its province is more factual than imaginative; hence its less exalted status.

In contrast to the imaginative representations of reality we expect in fiction, poetry, and drama, the essay embeds itself in the actual; it accumulates evidence and grapples with arguments; it dirties its hands with facts. Essays explain or explore a set of circumstances, persuading readers to see them in certain ways. Instead of the ambiguity and complexity associated with the other literary genres, the essay traffics in the direct and the explicit. Narrative or figurative language may be included, but it's there mostly to illustrate, dramatize, or otherwise explain an idea or argue a position.

To acknowledge the primacy of idea in the essay, however, is not to deny that essays can be imaginative, visionary, literary. Reading an essay with attention only to its information and ideas while ignoring its voice and style diminishes the pleasure it can provide.

Like the other literary genres, the essay invites and gratifies active, deliberative reading; it repays attention to voice and tone, style and structure, language and form. The essay rewards listening to writers and thinking along with them; their twists and turns of mind can surprise and delight, as well as inform and move. A great essay, Cecilia Watson reminds us, "puts on display the seemingly natural movement of the author's thoughts" (124). The key word here is "seemingly," as in reality writers expend considerable effort to discover, shape, and edit their prose to achieve that sense of naturalness.

One of the essay's pleasures for writers is the opportunity to clarify their thinking, figure out what they think, and make sense of their experience. One of its pleasures for us readers is to respond to the writer's thought and, in the process, discover what we think as well. In reading essays, we weigh what writers say and show against what we feel and know, measuring their attitudes, perspectives, beliefs, and values against our own.

Well-written essays reward considered, thoughtful reading. When we are most engaged with an essay, we make our reading a conversation with the writer. We listen and we learn; we consider and evaluate. We remain silent; we interrupt; we talk back. At its best, such engaged reading spurs not only our critical powers but our imaginative capacities as well. By entering into such imagined conversations with writers, we become fellow essayists, trying on and trying out ways of thinking about the writer's subject—essaying it along with the writer.

Here are a few kinds of conversations essays stimulate:

- A conversation with the text of the essay itself—our response to it, our interpretation, and our evaluation of it.
- A conversation with the writer, who is beyond the text while yet embodied in it.
- An imagined sense of who the writer is and why he or she may have written the essay we are reading.
- A conversation with ourselves—our changes of mind, shifts of direction, reconsiderations of the essayist's

meaning and idea, and of our own thinking and feelings in response to those.

- A conversation with others about what we read— whether others see what we see, and whether or not they agree with the writer and/or with us.

We might consider, further, how this set of conversations we have as readers can also be viewed from the perspective of the writer: the writer's conversation with her subject; the writer's conversation with her readers; the writer's conversation with herself; the writer's conversation with her reading (which may have prompted her writing in the first place).

Reading essays is a lot like reading other forms of literature. Some essays are much like short fiction because they tell stories; they use narrative structures, though the stories such essays narrate tend to be more factual than fictional. Langston Hughes's "Salvation" and Zora Neale Hurston's "How It Feels to Be Colored Me" are two noteworthy examples. Narrative essays such as these lay out their ideas explicitly, unlike fictional stories, which work largely by implication and suggestion rather than through direct statement and explanation. When narrative essays include fictional anecdotal evidence, those stories serve the primacy of the essay's idea.

Some essays share with poems highly charged language, especially figurative language, including imagery, simile, and metaphor. This affiliation, however, is only approximate, as poets typically write about one thing in terms of another, whereas essayists are generally more literal in conveying a sense of their subjects and ideas. Essayists tend to use figurative language to clarify and explain ideas.

The Essay Spectrum

Some essays are more descriptive than explanatory, and some convey ideas obliquely rather than directly. We can position essays on a *spectrum* ranging from narrative essays that feature anecdote and personal experience, on one end, to formal arguments that rely on syllogistic reasoning and other strategies of argumentation on the other. In between these poles we can place exploratory essays and expository essays, which are sometimes analytical, along with speculative and argumentative essays. The essay spectrum reflects the range of purposes essays advance: to tell stories and chronicle events; explore concepts and feelings; explain ideas and attitudes; make claims and present supporting evidence.

Not every essay sets out to confirm a claim; an essay is not necessarily an argument driven by an explicit thesis. Essays range widely in tone and form; speculative essays, especially, rarely exhibit a clear-cut, easily identifiable structure, but rather present a looser form less indebted to conventional organization patterns such as problem-solution, comparison-contrast, or classification and division. Speculative essays are journeys, excursions into thought, which don't necessarily arrive at a destination or resolve a clearly defined problem.

Argumentative essays differ in providing evidence to support their claims. In reading essays with a clear argumentative intent, we evaluate the nature and quantity of that evidence as well as how the writer deploys it, where and how various forms of evidence appear, how they relate to one another and to the essay's overall argument. Evidentiary support takes many forms: facts, statistics, data, examples, anecdotes, analogies, and more. Opposing viewpoints need to be acknowledged and discredited, if an argumentative essay is to be persuasive. Concessions may need to be granted.

Midway between the formality and directness of the argumentative essay and the less formal and explicit character of the speculative essay are narrative and expository essays. Readers respond readily to narrative essays; they enjoy stories, including the mostly factual stories in narrative essays.

Narrative essays are sometimes confused with fictional short stories. But essay writers and storytellers use narrative differently. Essayists employ narrative to advance, elaborate, illustrate, dramatize, or otherwise clarify an idea. Fictional short stories include narrative detail for its own sake; the story per se takes precedence over any idea we may derive from it. It's a matter of emphasis.

Orwell's "Shooting an Elephant," for example, consists largely of the story of how Orwell (or a fictional narrator) shot an elephant. It is based on Orwell's experience as a police inspector in Burma. Although the incident possesses considerable interest as a story, Orwell's primary purpose in telling it (whether pure fact or part fiction) is to advance an idea about imperialism. That idea Orwell presents explicitly midway through the narrative portion of the essay, and he returns to his idea in the essay's conclusion.

Narrative and argumentative essays differ from expository essays, which also advance ideas, but with less insistence than argumentative essays. And although expository essays may contain narrative elements, those narrative sections are typically briefer and less developed in expository essays than in narrative essays. The purpose of expository essays is explanation, to make something clear for readers, a characteristic they share with narrative essays. Once again, however, it's a matter of emphasis regarding the nature, quantity, and use of narrative that distinguishes exposition from other essay modes. In expository essays narrative augments other purposes, including speculation, explanation, or argument. More often than not, essayists mix modes, combining narration with exposition, or using exposition and narration in the service of an overarching explicit argument.

Essayists devise and design their essays; they discover their form, making use of whatever organizational patterns and strategies suit their purposes, audiences, and occasions. Whatever our experience in reading an essay, and whatever its author's purpose in writing it, ultimately an essay attempts to formulate a thought, explore it, work out its implications, and communicate the writer's thinking to readers.

The essay relishes and enshrines thinking. We read essays and write them to discover what others think so we can better see what we think. We read them for the intellectual stimulation they provide. We write them to experience a deep-rooted process of slow, playful (and sometimes painful) discovery. The essay involves exploration, inquiry, invitation, and provocation toward considered and deliberative thinking. It is much more than an attempt to make a case or prove a point.

Essays, however, also convey writers' feelings and attitudes, their impulses and lived experience. The inventor of the essay, Michel de Montaigne, discovered himself, revealed himself, and communicated his idiosyncratic way of being in the world in his *Essais*, first published in 1580, and then revised and expanded in 1582, 1587, 1588, and 1592, the year of his death. As James Olney points out, Montaigne's essays are a "quest that may give answers but no Answer, discoveries but no Discovery, truths but no Truth" (64). Montaigne's essays, and the best of the essays inspired by his example written over the centuries, offer us insights into how we might conduct our lives, what we might value and why; they provoke us to think about matters of human interest and engagement, without telling us what to think or what to do. Montaigne, in his essays, and those whose essays follow in his wake, offer ways to create and re-create ourselves, to find ourselves, to discover what matters most to us, and why.

The word "essay," from the French *essayer* (originally *essaier* in Renaissance French), means to try or attempt. An essay is an attempt to explore an idea, to discover its implications, and to convey something of the thinking process and the resulting idea to readers. In *A Literary Education*, Joseph Epstein, a committed essayist, describes the personal essay as a "form of discovery," in which the essayist finds out where he or she "stands on complex issues, problems, questions, subjects," in the process testing "feelings, instincts, and thoughts in the crucible of composition" (381). David Mikics notes, in *Slow Reading in a Hurried Age*, how "essays drift, turn sharply this way or that, run up a blind alley and stay there for a while" (291). He suggests, further, that essays rely upon a "partnership" (291) between readers and essay writers. We follow essayists' meanderings because essayists engage us, entertain us, surprise us, and, at their best, enlighten us.

The essay is a congenial genre, one easy to enjoy. The elements of the essay are familiar from everyday speech, an essay's voice conveying a mind's meanderings. An accommodating genre that embraces everything writers can imagine putting into it, the essay is well suited to the changing directions of a writer's thinking, adapting to the shifts in his or her feelings. Although the essay may lack the sonic sweetness and tart astringency of poetry, those tastes can be found among the works of essayists as well. Though the essay may not highlight the thrusting and counterthrusting stichomythic debate of ancient Greek tragic dialogue or Shakespearean comic repartee, essays bear their own styles of opposition. And if the essay as a genre does not conjure the imaginative worlds fiction writers typically create, essayists demonstrate a plenitude of imaginative possibilities—in voice and style, form and structure, image and idea. There is no one final, absolute, definite way to define, limit, and explain what an essay is and does and is capable of being and doing. The essay is a protean form.

Elements of the Essay

When we read an essay, it's useful to consider its basic elements: voice and tone, style, structure, and thought. Because each of these elements coexists with the others, each should be considered in relation to the others and in the context of the work as a whole—whether a speculative or narrative essay, an expository or exploratory essay, or an argumentative one.

Voice and Tone

We begin with the most immediate of an essay's characteristics: its voice and tone. When we read an essay, we hear a writer's voice; it's as if someone is speaking to us. The voice we hear may be commanding or collusive, friendly or angry, intimate, reserved, witty, authoritative, didactic, humorous—or a range of other possibilities. A writer's voice is our key to the essay's tone, the author's attitude toward the subject. Consider the voice of George Orwell in the first sentences of "Some Thoughts on the Common Toad."

> Before the swallow, before the daffodil, and not much later than the snowdrop, the common toad salutes the coming of spring after his own fashion, which is to emerge from a hole in the ground, where he has lain buried since the previous autumn, and crawl as rapidly as possible towards the nearest suitable patch of water. Something—some kind of shudder

in the earth, or perhaps merely a rise of a few degrees in the temperature—has told him that it is time to wake up: though a few toads appear to sleep the clock round and miss out a year from time to time—at any rate, I have more than once dug them up, alive and apparently well, in the middle of the summer.

What can we say about this essay's opening paragraph? We note, surely, its matter-of-fact tone. We sense someone speaking about something he cares about and pays considerable attention to. The writer shares his experience with us. He provides information in a direct and natural manner. His use of "perhaps" and "at any rate" help create an informal tone; his inclusion of specific details about toad behavior provides a sense of authority and expertise, such that we can trust what he says. The writer seems knowledgeable and thus credible.

Orwell describes rather than prescribes, and he writes in a middle linguistic register—neither overly formal nor catchily informal. Where some writers talk *at* us, Orwell talks *to* us, even *with* us. Some writers, such as Francis Bacon and Michel de Montaigne, reference literature and history heavily in their essays; Orwell's "Some Thoughts on the Common Toad," instead, emphasizes experience (though in other essays, Orwell writes about literature and history). For a contrast in an essayist's voice and tone, consider Francis Bacon's "Of Revenge," the complete essay a single dense paragraph.

REVENGE is a kind of wild justice; which the more man's nature runs to, the more ought law to weed it out. For as for the first wrong, it doth but offend the law; but the revenge of that wrong putteth the law out of office. Certainly, in taking revenge, a man is but even with his enemy; but in passing it over, he is superior; for it is a prince's part to pardon. And Solomon, I am sure, saith, *It is the glory of a man to pass by an offence.* That which is past is gone, and irrevocable; and wise men have enough to do with things present and to come; therefore they do but trifle with themselves, that labor in past matters. There is no man doth a wrong for the wrong's sake; but thereby to purchase himself profit, or pleasure, or honor, or the like. Therefore why should I be angry with a man for loving himself better than me? And if any man should do wrong merely out of ill-nature, why, yet it is but like the thorn or briar, which prick and scratch, because they can do no other. The most tolerable sort of revenge is for those wrongs which there is no law to remedy; but then let a man take heed the revenge be such as there is no law to punish; else a man's enemy is still beforehand, and it is two for one. Some, when they take revenge, are desirous the party should know whence it cometh. This is the more generous. For the delight seemeth to be not so much in doing the hurt as in making the party repent. But base and crafty cowards are like the arrow that flieth in the dark. Cosmus, duke of Florence, had a desperate saying against perfidious or neglecting friends, as if those wrongs were unpardonable; *You shall read* (saith he) *that we are commanded to forgive our enemies; but you never read that we are commanded to forgive our friends.* But yet the spirit of Job was in a better tune: *Shall we* (saith he) *take good at God's hands, and not be content to take evil also?* And so of friends in a proportion. This is certain, that a man that studieth revenge keeps his own wounds green, which otherwise would heal and do well. Public revenges are for the most part fortunate; as that for the death of Cæsar; for the death of Pertinax; for the death of Henry the Third of France; and many more. But in private revenges it is not so. Nay rather, vindictive persons live the life of witches; who, as they are mischievous, so end they infortunate.

Bacon's formal voice in this essay, as in most of his essays, is authoritative and impersonal. Absent is Orwell's direct address to us as "you." Bacon's voice is more annunciatory than Orwell's; Bacon's voice proclaims rather than describes. The few details and examples Bacon includes reference literature and history rather than everyday life. Books and historical figures are presented authoritatively, as prima facie evidence; those references reflect and embody a voice detached from experience, one less familiar and intimate, more reserved and distant than the voice we hear in "Some Thoughts on the Common Toad."

Of course, we hear many other kinds of voices in essays than those represented here by Orwell and Bacon. Consider the following sample of essayists' voices.

French toys: one could not find a better illustration of the fact that the adult Frenchman sees the child as another self. All the toys one commonly sees are essentially a microcosm of the adult world.

—"TOYS," ROLAND BARTHES (*MYTHOLOGIES*)

At three or four o'clock in the afternoon, the hour of *café con leche*, the women of my family gathered in Mamá's living room to speak of important things and retell familiar stories meant to be overheard by us young girls, their daughters.

—"CASA: A PARTIAL REMEMBRANCE OF A PUERTO RICAN CHILDHOOD," JUDITH ORTIZ COFER

Consider the hummingbird for a long moment. A hummingbird's heart beats ten times a second. A hummingbird's heart is the size of a pencil eraser. A hummingbird's heart is a lot of the hummingbird.

—"JOYAS VOLADORAS," BRIAN DOYLE

In those days it was either live with music or die with noise, and we chose rather desperately to live. In the process our apartment—what with its booby-trappings of audio equipment, wires, discs and tapes—came to resemble the Collier mansion, but that was later. First, there was the neighborhood, assorted drunks and a singer.

—"LIVING WITH MUSIC," RALPH ELLISON

He worked himself to death, finally and precisely, at 3:00 A.M. Sunday morning. The obituary didn't say that, of course. It said that he died of a coronary thrombosis—I think that was it—but everyone among his friends and acquaintances knew it instantly.

—"THE COMPANY MAN," ELLEN GOODMAN

I was saved from sin when I was going on thirteen. But not really saved. It happened like this.

—"SALVATION," LANGSTON HUGHES

I am colored but I offer nothing in the way of extenuating circumstances except the fact that I am the only Negro in the United States whose grandfather on the mother's side was *not* an Indian chief.

—"HOW IT FEELS TO BE COLORED ME,"
ZORA NEALE HURSTON

For the Greeks, beauty was a virtue: a kind of excellence. Persons then were assumed to be what we now have to call—lamely, enviously—*whole* persons. If it did occur to the Greeks to distinguish between a person's "inside" and "outside," they still expected that inner beauty would be matched by beauty of the other kind.

—"A WOMAN'S BEAUTY—PUT-DOWN OR POWER SOURCE?"
SUSAN SONTAG

I heartily accept the motto, "That government is best which governs least"; and I should like to see it acted up to more rapidly and systematically. Carried out, it finally amounts to this, which also I believe—"That government is best which governs not at all"; and when men are prepared for it, that will be the kind of government which they will have.

—"CIVIL DISOBEDIENCE," HENRY DAVID THOREAU

I'm here because I was born here and thus ruined for anywhere else. But I don't know about you.

—"CITY LIMITS," COLSON WHITEHEAD

First I write a sentence. I get a tickle of an idea for how the words might come together, like an angler feeling a tug on the rod's line. Then I sound out the sentence in my head. Then I tap it on my keyboard, trying to recall its shape. Then I look at it and say it aloud, to see if it sings.

—"A PEDANT'S APOLOGY," JOE MORAN

Style

Montaigne's essay style differs strikingly from that of Francis Bacon, and thus the experience of reading Montaigne's essays differs dramatically from the experience of reading Bacon's. Like Bacon's essays, Montaigne's range over a wide variety of topics, which typically include his personal experience as well as quotations from his reading. Provided below is one of Montaigne's briefest essays (his longest, "Apology for Raymond Sebond" constitutes a small book). "Of Smells" represents the style and method Montaigne employed consistently in the first of his three books of essays.

Of Smells

It is said of some, as of Alexander the Great, that their sweat emitted a sweet odor, owing to some rare and extraordinary constitution of theirs, of which Plutarch and others seek the cause. But the common make-up of bodies is the opposite, and the best condition they may have is to be free from smell. The sweetness even of the purest breath has nothing more excellent about it than to be without any odor that offends us, as is that of very healthy children. That is why, says Plautus:

A woman smells good when she does not smell.

The most perfect smell for a woman is to smell of nothing, as they say that her actions smell best when they are imperceptible and mute. And perfumes are rightly considered suspicious in those who use them, and thought to be used to cover up some natural defect in that quarter. Whence arise these nice sayings of the ancient poets: To smell good is to stink.

> You laugh at us because we do not smell.
> I'd rather smell of nothing than smell sweet.

MARTIAL

And elsewhere:

> Men who smell always sweet, Posthumus, don't smell good.

MARTIAL

However, I like very much to be surrounded with good smells, and I hate bad ones beyond measure, and detect them from further off than anyone else:

> My scent will sooner be aware
> Where goat-smells, Polypus, in hairy arm-pits lurk,
> Than keen hounds scent a wild boar's lair.

HORACE

The simplest and most natural smells seem to me the most agreeable. And this concern chiefly affects the ladies. Amidst the densest barbarism, the Scythian women, after washing, powder and plaster their whole body and face with a certain odoriferous drug that is native to their soil; and having removed this paint to approach the men, they find themselves both sleek and perfumed.

Whatever the odor is, it is a marvel how it clings to me and how apt my skin is to imbibe it. He who complains of nature that she has left man without an instrument to convey smells to his nose is wrong, for they convey themselves. But in my particular case my mustache, which is thick, performs that service. If I bring my gloves or my handkerchief near it, the smell will stay there a whole day. It betrays the place I come from. The close kisses of youth, savory, greedy, and sticky, once used to adhere to it and stay there for several hours after. And yet, for all that, I find myself little subject to epidemics, which are caught by communication and bred by the contagion of the air; and I have escaped those of my time, of which there have been many sorts in our cities and our armies. We read of Socrates that though he never left Athens during many occurrences of the plague which so many times tormented that city, he alone never found himself the worse for it.

The doctors might, I believe, derive more use from odors than they do; for I have often noticed that they make a change in me and work upon my spirits according to their properties; which makes me approve of the idea that the use of incense and perfumes in churches, so ancient and widespread in all nations and religions, was intended to delight us and arouse and purify our senses to make us more fit for contemplation.

I should like, in order to judge of it, to have shared the art of those cooks who know how to add a seasoning of foreign odors to the savor of foods, as was particularly remarked in the service of the king of Tunis, who in our time landed at Naples to confer with the Emperor Charles. They stuffed his foods with aromatic substances, so sumptuously that one peacock and two pheasants came to a hundred ducats to dress them in that manner; and when they were carved, they filled not only the dining hall, but all the rooms in his palace, and even the neighboring houses, with sweet fumes which did not vanish for some time.

The principal care I take in my lodgings is to avoid heavy, stinking air. Those beautiful cities Venice and Paris weaken my fondness for them, by the acrid smell of the marshes of the one and of the mud of the other.

Readers are often surprised that an essayist can speak so familiarly about his experience, can present so much about himself in the process of exploring a topic such as smell. Like Bacon, Montaigne read widely in the literature and history of antiquity, in Latin especially. Unlike Bacon, however, Montaigne connects his reading directly with his experience of living. The two are mixed in "Of Smells," with the quotations from Montaigne's reading of poetry set off and identified. His references to history—to the Scythian women and the king of Tunis, for example—lack that information.

In reading "Of Smells" and considering Montaigne's response to different smells, including his own odors, we open the door to the types of smells we ourselves may find enticing or offensive. Montaigne captures the sensuous nature of olfactory experience, how smells stay with us and stick to us. He remembers, through smell, the sensual and sticky quality of kisses, and the way smell extends their impact. We know, today, how important smell is for our ability to taste, something especially important to Montaigne, as he described his essays, overall, as ways to "taste" his experiences, to ascertain their distinctive qualities through sampling the many ways they appeal to his intellectual, emotional, and experiential palette.

A writer's style derives from choices of diction, syntax, and figurative language—for starters. Style refers to a writer's choices and arrangements of words to create his or her verbal identity, an identity as distinctive as one's face, voice, or fingerprint. A writer's style reflects and represents a unique way of perceiving the world and of conveying that perception to readers. At once the most distinctive and elusive aspect of a writer's work, style conveys the writer's world in all its subtlety, nuance, and distinctiveness. Each writer imagines the world he or she creates; no other writer imagines and renders it in just that way.

A taste of authorial essay styles is included in the samples in the previous section on voice. Here, however, we take a closer look at a pair of writers whose styles overlap in some respects and diverge in others. Both are eminent essayists, as well as writers of fiction; each possesses a distinctive style; each has written memorable essays—James Baldwin and Alice Walker. First, we'll look at and listen to a paragraph about Baldwin's father from his essay, "Notes of a Native Son."

> He was, I think, very handsome. I gather this from photographs and from my own memories of him, dressed in his Sunday best and on his way to preach a sermon somewhere, when I was little. Handsome, proud, and ingrown, "like a

toe-nail," somebody said. But he looked to me, as I grew older, like pictures I had seen of African tribal chieftains: he really should have been naked, with war-paint on and barbaric mementos, standing among spears. He could be chilling in the pulpit and indescribably cruel in his personal life and he was certainly the most bitter man I have ever met; yet it must be said that there was something else in him, buried in him, which lent him his tremendous power and, even, a rather crushing charm. It had something to do with his blackness, I think—he was very black—with his blackness and his beauty, and with the fact that he knew that he was black but did not know that he was beautiful. He claimed to be proud of his blackness but it had also been the cause of much humiliation and it had fixed bleak boundaries to his life. He was not a young man when we were growing up and he had already suffered many kinds of ruin; in his outrageously demanding and protective way he loved his children, who were black like him and menaced, like him; and all these things sometimes showed in his face when he tried, never to my knowledge with any success, to establish contact with any of us. When he took one of his children on his knee to play, the child always became fretful and began to cry; when he tried to help one of us with our homework the absolutely unabating tension which emanated from him caused our minds and our tongues to become paralyzed, so that he, scarcely knowing why, flew into a rage and the child, not knowing why, was punished. If it ever entered his head to bring a surprise home for his children, it was, almost unfailingly, the wrong surprise and even the big watermelons he often brought home on his back in the summertime led to the most appalling scenes. I do not remember, in all those years, that one of his children was ever glad to see him come home. From what I was able to gather of his early life, it seemed that this inability to establish contact with other people had always marked him and had been one of the things which had driven him out of New Orleans. There was something in him, therefore, groping and tentative, which was never expressed and which was buried with him. One saw it most clearly when he was facing new people and hoping to impress them. But he never did, not for long. . . . He had lived and died in an intolerable bitterness of spirit and it frightened me . . . to realize that this bitterness was now mine.

Where to begin with this poignant portrait of Baldwin's sad father? What accounts for the power of Baldwin's prose here? How does he convey the reality of his father's presence, both his father's power and his failure, his strength and his ineptitude?

The style in this passage is formal, dignified, elegant, allusive. Baldwin writes about his father and their (non)relationship, and about the environment in which they both lived. He writes personally but not casually. Even though he uses "I" and "we," "me" and "mine," Baldwin's solemn tone is evident in his elevated diction: "unabating" and "emanated," for example.

It's not through diction alone, however, that Baldwin achieves this solemn elegiac tone. Sentence rhythm enforces it. Baldwin interrupts the linear movement of his sentences by embedding words and phrases in a rising and falling motion. This rise and fall of the rhythm of Baldwin's prose adds to the gravity of his style.

- He was, I think, very handsome.
- But he looked to me, as I grew older, like pictures I had seen of African tribal chieftains.
- It had something to do with his blackness, I think—he was very black—with his blackness and his beauty, and with the fact that he knew that he was black but did not know that he was beautiful.
- If it ever entered his head to bring a surprise home for his children, it was, almost unfailingly, the wrong surprise. . . . I do not remember, in all those years, that one of his children was ever glad to see him come home.

In addition, Baldwin makes effective use of balanced syntax and of repetition to further reinforce his elevated tone: "He loved his children, who were black like him and menaced, like him." And:

"When he took one of his children on his knee to play, the child always became fretful and began to cry; when he tried to help one of us with our homework . . . he, scarcely knowing why, flew into a rage and the child, not knowing why, was punished." Baldwin's repetition of words ("black," "blackness," "beauty," "bitterness," and "pride" along with repeating parallel sentence structures throughout the paragraph contribute to both its grandeur and its pathos.

One way to appreciate Baldwin's style is to physically copy on page or screen these and other striking sentences. Copying slows us down to better notice the shapes and rhythms of his sentences. Another is to write imitations of some of them, using our own topics, and expressing our own ideas—while following the syntactic patterns and elevated diction Baldwin uses. Imitation was a common practice in the study of rhetoric in the Renaissance and seventeenth century. Shakespeare and Milton were taught writing through imitating the writers of classical antiquity.

But let's listen to a different tone, as Alice Walker describes her mother in the following passage from her essay "In Search of Our Mothers' Gardens."

And this is how I came to know my mother: she seemed a large, soft, loving-eyed woman who was rarely impatient in our home. Her quick, violent temper was on view only a few times a year, when she battled with the white landlord who had the misfortune to suggest to her that her children did not need to go to school.

She made all the clothes we wore, even my brothers' overalls. She made all the towels and sheets we used. She spent the summers canning vegetables and fruits. She spent the winter evenings making quilts enough to cover all our beds.

During the "working" day she labored beside—not behind—my father in the fields. Her day began before sunup, and did not end until late at night. There was never a moment for her to sit down, undisturbed, to unravel her own private thoughts; never a time free from interruption—by work or the noisy inquiries of her many children. And yet, it is to my mother—and all our mothers who were not famous—that I went in search of the secret of what has fed that muzzled and often mutilated, but vibrant creative spirit that the black woman has inherited, and that pops out in wild and unlikely places to this day.

. . . Before she left home for the fields, she watered her flowers, chopped up the grass, and laid out new beds. When she returned from the fields she might divide clumps of bulbs, dig a cold pit, uproot and replant roses, or prune branches from her taller bushes or trees—until night came and it was too dark to see.

Whatever she planted grew as if by magic, and her fame as a grower of flowers spread over three counties. Because of her creativity with her flowers, even my memories of poverty are seen through a screen of blooms—sunflowers, petunias, roses, dahlias, forsythia, spirea, delphiniums, verbena . . . and on and on.

And I remember people coming to my mother's yard to be given cuttings from her flowers; I hear again the praise showered on her because whatever rocky soil she landed on, she turned into a garden. A garden so brilliant with colors, so original in its design, so magnificent with life and creativity, that to this day people drive by our house in Georgia—perfect strangers and imperfect strangers—and ask to stand or walk among my mother's art.

I notice that it is only when my mother is working in her flowers that she is radiant, almost to the point of being invisible—except as Creator: hand and eye. She is involved in work her soul must have. Ordering the universe in the image of her personal conception of Beauty.

Like Baldwin, Walker writes in the first person about a parent. Her tone differs from his largely because her attitude contrasts with his. Walker's love for and appreciation of her mother shine through her prose; these feelings are especially evident in the details she includes about her mother. Walker's style is lighter, more informal than Baldwin's. She uses everyday speech, noting how her mother "battled" with the landlord, and how her temper was rarely "on view." She employs short simple sentences, such as "She made all the clothes we wore, even my brothers' overalls."

Walker's style also differs from Baldwin's in her use of sentence fragments. Walker uses fragments twice, both times at the end of a paragraph: "A garden so brilliant with colors . . . my mother's art"; "Ordering the universe in the image of her personal conception of Beauty." As a rhetorical strategy for achieving emphasis, the fragment can drive a fact or feeling across with intensity and power. Such features of Walker's writing make it more casual and intimate than Baldwin's. And though Walker is capable of writing long, intricate sentences, she achieves her brand of eloquence with different stylistic techniques. And so we can do with Walker's sentences what we did with Baldwin's—set them apart, copy and imitate them using our own topics and ideas.

One additional stylistic element to notice and perhaps also imitate in the writing of both Walker and Baldwin is their use of comparisons. Walker's garden reflects her mother's creativity. Walker describes the praise "showered" on her mother; she compares her flower growing and arranging to "art"; she describes her mother as a "Creator," with a capital C. Baldwin compares his father's fierce demeanor to that of an African warrior chieftain. In a less flattering comparison, he mentions that someone once likened his father to an ingrown toenail. And Baldwin emphasizes that his father had something "buried" in him that contributed to his power and "crushing charm" but that also had set "bleak boundaries" to his father's life.

Structure

The structural features of essays are not as immediately visible as the stanzas of poems or as conveniently laid out as the acts and scenes of plays. With essays we are interested more in the structure of the writer's thought, in the way an idea is developed. For most essays, regardless of their type—whether narrative or expository; exploratory, speculative, or argumentative—we attend to a basic three-part structure: beginning (or introduction); middle (or development); and ending (or conclusion). When analyzing essays, we identify, first, the end of the beginning and the beginning of the ending. We can then map out its middle, identify its parts, whether paragraphs or groups of paragraphs. Along with this, we can explain to ourselves what each of those middle sections is doing in the essay, and how each part is related to the parts before and after it.

Essays offer readers three essential characteristics: an interesting idea; evidence to support the idea; and a form in which the idea develops. If any one of these features is absent, there is no essay. Without one of these elements, a text might be an anecdote or memoir, a report or paper, but not an essay.

I prefer the word "idea" to "thesis" because" idea" suggests an openness and development of thought that "thesis" does not. "Thesis" suggests something to be proven or demonstrated. It carries overtones of an argument finished, closed, concluded once and for all. "Idea," on the other hand, suggests something to be explored, turned over in the minds of writer and readers, something unfinished about which there is more to say—offering a reader something interesting to think about.

I prefer "structure" and "form" to "organization" because organization suggests a systematic format, an outline or even a predetermined template—something on the order of the five-paragraph essay with its keyhole- or funnel-shaped introduction; its three middle paragraphs, each illustrating one of the paper's three supporting points; and a single concluding paragraph, which often repeats in summary fashion what was said earlier in the essay. This organizational pattern has its uses, certainly, but those uses are limited. "Structure" and "form" suggest ways ideas can be shaped, how ideas unfold and evolve.

I also prefer the term "evidence" to "proof" for similar reasons. "Proof" suggests something firmly established. Evidence, by contrast, is something to be weighed and considered, something worthy of deliberation and evaluation. We appraise the extent to which an essay's evidence is suitable, interesting, and persuasive. We consider the extent to which it is intellectually provocative and emotionally engaging, the extent to which it surprises us, as it may also have surprised the writer in discovering it.

Whatever their structural properties, whatever form they assume, essays serve readers as occasions for reflection; they stimulate thinking; and they serve as models for imitation in writing. Orwell structures "Shooting an Elephant" in hybrid fashion. He begins with description and narrative, developing the conflict he identifies in his opening paragraph. Just past the midpoint of the essay, however, Orwell shifts gears by moving into exposition; he explains the essay's central idea about the destructive consequences of colonialism. He provides this explanation in a single analytical paragraph that precedes a tour-de-force description at the story's (and essay's) climax—when the narrator pulls the trigger of his rifle, firing shot after shot into the elephant, with apparently little if any effect, until, finally, the elephant crashes to the ground. After this dramatic, climactic, and emotionally exhausting section, Orwell continues with the essay/story's denouement, a coda tinged with irony.

Bacon's "Of Revenge," which appears earlier in this chapter, is structured differently, appearing as a single block of print. No paragraph indents cue shifts of focus. But Bacon does provide a structure for his essay. The first major structural shift comes with the sentence "The most tolerable sort of revenge is for those wrongs which there is no law to remedy . . ." The eight sentences that precede that one do two related things: they suggest that it is better to avoid revenge (sentences 1–5), and they explain why some people commit wrongs against others (sentences 6–8). At this point, Bacon changes course, discussing different types of revenge, explaining why some kinds of revenge are preferable to others (sentences 9–12). We might consider this the middle of Bacon's essay, where he concedes that revenge does have some value. However, he doesn't remain in this mode for long. For the remainder of the essay, beginning with sentence 13, Bacon reverts to his earlier counsel: that revenge is destructive mostly to the avengers, keeping their "wounds green" and rendering their ends "infortunate." This last part, then, forms the essay's conclusion.

Thought

Edward Hoagland, an accomplished and prolific essayist, has described the essay as a work that "hangs somewhere on a line between two sturdy poles: this is what I think, and this is what I am"

(25). The sense of self provided by essay writers manifests itself in their styles and voices—Hoagland's "what I am." With Hoagland's "what I think," essayists convey their ideas, attitudes, and values; they speak to their readers "mind to mind."

In choosing to write essays, a writer exhibits an interest in being factual rather than fictional. The choice of fact over fiction testifies to the writer's concern for expressing an idea. Even when essayists rely heavily on narrative to convey feelings and attitudes, as Orwell does in "Shooting an Elephant," their emphasis ultimately rests upon an idea. It is the primacy of idea that makes an essay what it is.

Here, now, is Orwell's pivotal idea paragraph from "Shooting an Elephant":

But at that moment I glanced round at the crowd that had followed me. It was an immense crowd, two thousand at the least and growing every minute. It blocked the road for a long distance on either side. I looked at the sea of yellow faces above the garish clothes—faces all happy and excited over this bit of fun, all certain that the elephant was going to be shot. They were watching me as they would watch a conjurer about to perform a trick. They did not like me, but with the magical rifle in my hands I was momentarily worth watching. And suddenly I realized that I should have to shoot the elephant after all. The people expected it of me and I had got to do it; I could feel their two thousand wills pressing me forward, irresistibly. And it was at this moment, as I stood there with the rifle in my hands, that I first grasped the hollowness, the futility of the white man's dominion in the East. Here was I, the white man with his gun, standing in front of the unarmed native crowd—seemingly the leading actor of the piece; but in reality I was only an absurd puppet pushed to and fro by the will of those yellow faces behind. I perceived in this moment that when the white man turns tyrant it is his own freedom that he destroys. He becomes a sort of hollow, posing dummy, the conventionalized figure of a sahib. For it is the condition of his rule that he shall spend his life in trying to impress the 'natives', and so in every crisis he has got to do what the 'natives' expect of him. He wears a mask, and his face grows to fit it. I had got to shoot the elephant. I had committed myself to doing it when I sent for the rifle. A sahib has got to act like a sahib; he has got to appear resolute, to know his own mind and do definite things. To come all that way, rifle in hand, with two thousand people marching at my heels, and then to trail feebly away, having done nothing—no, that was impossible. The crowd would laugh at me. And my whole life, every white man's life in the East, was one long struggle not to be laughed at.

In this paragraph, Orwell interrupts his story about the elephant to explain the significance of the experience, which is in part that imperialism is destructive of both the oppressed and the oppressors. Orwell does not make this point either abstractly or generally. Instead, he presents it within a specific context: the shooting of an elephant in Burma in the 1930s by a British colonial official. To increase the impact of his idea, Orwell employs irony and imagery.

In analyzing Orwell's paragraph, we should consider who is in charge in this scene. Who has the power and who seems to have the power? How does Orwell help us understand the irony of this power reversal? Where does he make his point about this power shift most directly?

That Orwell is at the mercy of the people he seems to be leading is ironic enough. But he underscores that irony through imagery: "the leading actor" is an "absurd puppet," with "actor" indicating his performed role (unintended but nonetheless inescapable), and "puppet" his lack of control. Orwell further reinforces his idea through the image of the "mask," which extends the theatrical imagery.

That mask image, moreover, conveys a further complication of Orwell's idea: that although a person may originally keep himself distinct from a role he performs, at some point he may, indeed, *become* what he initially only pretended to be. "He wears a mask," Orwell writes, "and his face grows to fit it." What was at first a role played in a drama can become an aspect of an individual's identity and a mark of his character.

This more interesting and complex idea leads forcefully into Orwell's statement that "when the white man turns tyrant it is his own freedom that he destroys." It doesn't get more explicit and more political than this. It is ironic, of course, that in gaining power over others one loses one's freedom. This paradoxical idea lies at the heart of this centrally located and vitally important paragraph and represents the key idea of the essay overall.

A final point about idea is that thinking exists in relation to feeling. An essayist's thoughts are intertwined with emotion. A writer's thinking emanates from his or her feelings, has its basis in feeling. Alice Walker's "In Search of Our Mothers' Gardens" and James Baldwin's "Notes of a Native Son" illustrate powerfully felt thought, feeling conveyed with intellectual passion and incisive intelligence.

The Interpretive Impulse

Interpretation is a dynamic act of thinking and an ongoing one. We make sense of a text as we read it; we make additional or alternative sense of it as we reflect on it later. Interpretation of any text is formed and re-formed as we read and think, reread and rethink.

Here is an opportunity to engage further in the act of interpretation with the first two paragraphs of Joan Didion's essay, "Los Angeles Notebook." In this paragraph and in the essay overall, Didion works by implication rather than by stating things explicitly. She expects her readers to make inferences based on the details she provides. To make those inferences, we make connections among the details we observe.

Here is Didion's opening paragraph:

> There is something uneasy in the Los Angeles air this afternoon, some unnatural stillness, some tension. What it means is that tonight a Santa Ana will begin to blow, a hot wind from the northeast whining down through the Cajon and San Gorgonio Passes, blowing up sand storms out along Route

66, drying the hills and the nerves to flash point. For a few days now we will see smoke back in the canyons, and hear sirens in the night. I have neither heard nor read that a Santa Ana is due, but I know it, and almost everyone I have seen today knows it too. We know it because we feel it. The baby frets. The maid sulks. I rekindle a waning argument with the telephone company, then cut my losses and lie down, given over to whatever it is in the air. To live with the Santa Ana is to accept, consciously or unconsciously, a deeply mechanistic view of human behavior.

To begin to make sense of this paragraph, we highlight words and phrases that contribute to its tone and mood. We identify details that lead Didion to surmise that a Santa Ana wind is coming. After establishing those more basic, factual elements of the paragraph, we can consider what Didion means when she writes that the hot, dry wind of the Santa Ana dries out not just the hills, but people's nerves, as well. We need to understand what she means by "a mechanistic view of human behavior." We have an incipient sense about those things from the start. But we acquire a clearer sense of what they imply and mean as we read on, and as we read back into this first paragraph, analyzing its language and detail in relationship to the language and detail Didion includes as the essay progresses. We'll look at just one additional paragraph, the second of the essay.

I recall being told, when I first moved to Los Angeles and was living on an isolated beach, that the Indians would throw themselves into the sea when the bad wind blew. I could see why. The Pacific turned ominously glossy during a Santa Ana period, and one woke in the night troubled not only by the peacocks screaming in the olive trees but by the eerie absence of surf. The heat was surreal. The sky had a yellow cast, the kind of light sometimes called "earthquake weather." My only neighbor would not come out of her house for days, and there were no lights at night, and her husband roamed the place with a machete. One day he would tell me that he had heard a trespasser, the next a rattlesnake.

The key to interpretation is to identify relationships, to understand how one paragraph, one sentence, one detail, one image, connects with another. And so here we need to identify the relationship between Didion's two paragraphs. How does Didion's second paragraph relate to her first? What does this second paragraph of "Los Angeles Notebook" *do*? Didion's second paragraph presents two kinds of details—details about the external world and details about human behavior. Once we understand this, we can consider what the two types of details have in common, and how these new details are related to those of the first paragraph.

What do the accumulated details suggest in terms of the essay's developing idea? What do they contribute to the essay's thought? And what kinds of thinking do they provoke in us as we read?

In order to answer those questions, we need to look closely at Didion's style. We've begun doing this, of course, but we need to drill down a bit further. How do her choices among words, her sentence patterns, images, allusions, and comparisons work together with her anecdotes and selection of detail to convey her tone and establish her idea?

Didion's diction conveys the tensions that emerge among people in Los Angeles when a Santa Ana arrives. She writes, for example, that there is something "uneasy" in the air, that there is an "unnatural" stillness. She further describes its ominousness as "*whatever is in the air.*" The vagueness here is deliberate; the mysterious cause of the tension increases the intensity of people's reactions. That intensity and anxiety are reflected in other aspects of Didion's language, such as her description of the sea as "ominously glossy" with an "eerie absence of surf"; of the heat as "surreal": and of "earthquake weather."

It's no wonder people are on edge.

Besides her striking diction, Didion includes a selection of anecdotal evidence—details to suggest how weather provokes people's strange behavior. She mentions how Indians would throw themselves into the sea during a Santa Ana, how a resident stays in a dark house, unwilling to come outside. She notes how a man roams his yard with a machete. In subsequent paragraphs, she describes fights breaking out, murders contemplated. And she reports on the high incidence of accidents and deaths during the time of the hot dry Santa Ana. Putting together our observations about Didion's diction and selection of detail, we begin to see how Didion creates a sense of foreboding, of impending catastrophe.

The form of Didion's sentences reinforces her argument. Didion employs repetition of a phrase in parallel structure: "something uneasy," "some unnatural stillness," "some tension." She balances sentences and keeps them short for a strong, hard-hitting effect: "I know it . . . everyone . . . knows it . . . We know it . . . we feel it." She also varies the length of her sentences and diversifies their forms. The short sentences in the opening paragraph are effective partly because they follow a series of longer ones. The contrast of long with short strikes us forcibly, conveying Didion's sense of certainty and establishing her authority.

The comparisons Didion uses are mostly metaphors. She mentions an incendiary dryness that dries people's "nerves" to the "flash point," when they "rekindle . . . argument." The incendiary dryness is both literal and metaphorical. Literally, it is so dry when the Santa Ana blows that spontaneous combustion can occur. Fires simply break out from the combined effects of intense dryness and heat. But the concept of flash point has implications for human behavior as well. Although "flash point" is literally the temperature at which an object can burst spontaneously into flames, metaphorically, it is the point at which human beings lose control and burst into acts of violence and destruction.

Didion does more, however, than create a sense of ominousness and catastrophe. In her selection of diction and detail, she helps us see just how powerfully weather can affect people's behavior. Her accumulation of details is unrelenting. She piles them up in an attempt to persuade us that there is a "mechanistic" quality to human behavior, to convince us that we are conditioned by aspects of weather, that we are at the mercy of nature's forces, that we are less in control of our moods and behavior than we think.

Didion's essay, however, is not a traditional argument, a logical attempt at persuasion. Her method is different: it's oblique, indirect, an invitation to consider the implications of her accumulating details, and not an explicit argument. To that end, Didion includes not merely historical and scientific "facts" (in subsequent paragraphs not excerpted here), but also hearsay and anecdote, along with her personal experience.

Didion is a witness; she serves as our eyes and ears. By mixing objective evidence with her subjective impressions, she makes a strong case for her implied argument, a case that pulls us in emotionally as well as intellectually. By accumulating a wide range of diverse kinds of information and detail—historical, scientific, statistical, personal, and anecdotal—she solidifies her idea and intensifies our experience of what living with the Santa Ana is like.

Reading Longer Works

To what extent can we apply the strategies used for brief and mid-length essays to much longer ones, to book-length essays such as Michel de Montaigne's "Apology for Raymond Sebond," James Baldwin's *The Fire Next Time*, and Rebecca Solnit's *Men Explain Things to Me*? How might we go about reading book-length essays like these?

One approach, of course, would be to analyze the text via the literary elements of voice and tone, style, structure, and thought. These traditional ways in to nonfiction yield insights into a writer's craft and a book's argument—to both what is being claimed or said, and how the writer conveys his or her idea and presents supporting evidence.

Another approach is to focus on the work's opening, a practice useful for reading a longish work in any genre, from an epic poem to a long play such as *Man and Superman* or *Angels in America*, to a substantial novel such as *Middlemarch* or *War and Peace*.

In reading a nonfiction prose work of significant length and complexity such as *The Education of Henry Adams* or *Democracy in America*, for example, or *The Decline and Fall of the Roman Empire*, we can work through a close reading of the first few pages or chapters to get a feel for the book's language and texture and tone, to become acquainted with its narrator, style, and milieu. If the work is heavy on dialogue, we might imagine how it would sound, to hear the interplay of the book's voices. If the book relies more on descriptive detail, we can inquire into the nature and value of the writer's purpose in including it. A close look at a work's beginning gives us a chance to absorb key structural, stylistic, and argumentative elements, while becoming familiar with its voice and tone and what may be distinctive about it.

A slow, attentive reading of a work's opening—whatever its length—also prepares readers to continue on their own. Working carefully through a book's beginning increases both the confidence and the interest necessary to proceed further. Reading slowly and attentively, what might we notice about the following excerpt from near the beginning of Ta-Nehisi Coates's book-length essay, *Between the World and Me*?

> I write you in your 15th year. I am writing you because this was the year you saw Eric Garner choked to death for selling cigarettes; because you know now that Renisha McBride was shot for seeking help, that John Crawford was shot down for browsing in a department store. And you have seen men in uniform drive by and murder Tamir Rice, a 12-year-old child whom they were oath-bound to protect. And you know now, if you did not before, that the police departments of your country have been endowed with the authority to destroy your body. It does not matter if the destruction is the result of an unfortunate overreaction. It does not matter if it originates in a misunderstanding. It does not matter if the destruction springs from a foolish policy. Sell cigarettes without the proper authority and your body can be destroyed. Turn into a dark stairwell and your body can be destroyed. The destroyers will rarely be held accountable. Mostly they will receive pensions.
>
> There is nothing uniquely evil in these destroyers or even in this moment. The destroyers are merely men enforcing the whims of our country, correctly interpreting its heritage and legacy. This legacy aspires to the shackling of black bodies. It is hard to face this. But all our phrasing—*race relations, racial chasm, racial justice, racial profiling, white privilege*, even *white supremacy*—serves to obscure that racism is a visceral experience, that it dislodges brains, blocks airways, rips muscle,

extracts organs, cracks bones, breaks teeth. You must never look away from this. You must always remember that the sociology, the history, the economics, the graphs, the charts, the regressions all land, with great violence, upon the body. And should one live in such a body? What should be our aim beyond meager survival of constant, generational, ongoing battery and assault? I have asked this question all my life. I have sought the answer through my reading and writings, through the music of my youth, through arguments with your grandfather, with your mother. I have searched for answers in nationalist myth, in classrooms, out on the streets, and on other continents. The question is unanswerable, which is not to say futile. The greatest reward of this constant interrogation, of confrontation with the brutality of my country, is that it has freed me from ghosts and myths.

COMMENTS

Coates's book began as an essay published in the *Atlantic*, where, for a time, Coates was a contributing editor. From its initial publication, the piece provoked response, mostly favorable, though not without some criticism. The essay's expanded book version won the 2015 National Book Award for nonfiction, and was in contention for the 2016 Pulitzer Prize for General Nonfiction, as well.

Coates offers advice in the form of a letter based on his personal experience; he warns his son about the kind of life he may very well live as a Black male in America. The book's dominant tone is cautionary, its style ranging from simple directness to passionate eloquence. Coates provides a profusion of precise detail to anchor his advice in the actual physical world he and his son inhabit. For Coates and for many African American men, that world is drenched in fear, a fear felt physically in the body, the bodies of Black men, who, as Coates reminds us, continue to suffer the effects of a socially systemic racism, which he describes as "a visceral experience, that . . . dislodges brains, blocks airways, rips muscle, extracts organs, cracks bones, breaks teeth."

Coates explores in his letter/lecture to his son how he, and by extension any Black male in America, can do something more than simply survive the "constant, generational, ongoing battery and assault." He does not offer any consolation; his vision of society, and of the challenge of living and not merely surviving in a world of rampant racism, is not encouraging. His outlook is based, of course, not only on his own experience, but also on a study of history, with its catalog of horrors, including slavery, reconstruction, Jim Crow, lynching, denial of voting rights, discrimination in housing, inequality in health, education, and general welfare, and all the rest.

Like James Baldwin, whose *The Fire Next Time* served as both inspiration and model for his essay and book, Coates presents compelling and overwhelming evidence for his claims. Here is Baldwin presenting a litany of America's failures: "a collection of myths to which white Americans cling: that their ancestors were all freedom-loving heroes, that they were born in the greatest country the world has ever seen, or that Americans are invincible in battle and wise in peace, that Americans have always dealt honorably with Mexicans and Indians and all other neighbors or inferiors" (*Fire* 101). Like Baldwin, as well, Coates elects to confront the oppression and dangers he catalogs head on. His is no attempt to seek accommodation or reconciliation; there is no interest in offering excuses and making reparations.

Throughout his brief but compelling book, Coates conveys the brutal facts of life for Black men like his son, so that his son and others can figure out, first, how to survive the dangerous threats to their bodies and their lives, and, second, how to live with some degree of dignity, fulfillment, and humanity. His solemn tone and bleak message are unrelenting.

Understanding these things about Coates's early paragraphs, we know what we are in for should we decide to continue reading. We understand that for Coates and his son, his advice in *Between the World and Me* encompasses matters of life and death. We understand, too, that his book will take us through much more than an exercise in intellectual comprehension. It will engage us emotionally as well. The beginning provides ample and harrowing evidence for that.

FOUR

Reading Fiction

LABORATORIES FOR THE CREATION OF THE SELF

The story itself becomes the truth, not just for the writer but for the reader.
—LUCIA BERLIN

Reading Fiction

What allure do stories hold for us? What are fiction's pleasures? We read stories largely for the emotional and intellectual pleasures they bring—being surprised or disturbed by an unexpected turn of events, being satisfied as our expectations are met, or perplexed when they are not. Well-told stories involve us in the lives of their characters. Stories enthrall us; their words and images bring characters and their passions to life. Stories provide us with the pleasure of recognition and the thrill of vicarious experience. They allow us to live in the minds and hearts and worlds of others, widening our circle of sympathy. Stories also increase our quotient of empathy.

Fiction affects us in still other ways. Stories entertain us with their plots, taking us on journeys of adventure and discovery. They instruct by showing us things we had not noticed or known, by helping us see things in new ways, perhaps from a different perspective or an alternate reality: "[W]hat if," asks Zadie Smith in *Feel Free*, "things were other than they are" (337)? Reading stories and novels enables us to experience life in many different realms. Doing so enlarges our own imaginative capacities, deepens our perception of the world, and enriches our understanding of other people. And although we can certainly gain information from reading fiction—information about history, for example, from Hilary Mantel's *Wolf Hall* and Tolstoy's *War and Peace*, about nineteenth-century science from Elizabeth Gilbert's *The Signature of All Things*, early twentieth-century Ireland from the novels and stories of James Joyce, and totalitarianism from George Orwell's *Animal*

Farm and *1984*—it is not for information, primarily, that we read these, or indeed any, works of fiction.

Stories both arouse and satisfy curiosity, a double motivation for reading fiction. We also read fiction to learn how to live, to learn what's possible, to be amused and amazed, transported and transformed emotionally, psychologically, even spiritually. In addition, stories help us understand ourselves, enabling us to make sense of where we have come from and how we have arrived. The title of Thomas Newkirk's *Minds Made for Stories* suggests the centrality of stories in our lives; through stories we explain ourselves to ourselves (22–28).

In reading fiction, we share the imaginative vision of another person, adopting, however briefly, his or her (or its) way of perceiving the world. Stories, thus, function as laboratories for the creation of a self. We learn through them how to become ourselves, in part, by trying on the roles of the characters we meet in fiction. Fiction serves us as a rehearsal for life.

Zadie Smith describes novel reading as a "leap into the possibility of another life" (340)—but also as a way of getting inside the minds of characters as they negotiate the complex network of decisions they make in their own fictional lives. Novels give us practice in making choices, and watching them play out in the fictive lives of others instead of in our own actual lives. One example from many: the character of Dorothea Brooke in George Eliot's *Middlemarch*, who makes a bad decision in choosing whom to marry. Dorothea's passionate idealism leads her to marry a dry-as-dust scholar, Edward Casaubon, who hopes to create a grand synthesis of universal knowledge—the "Key to All Mythologies." The novel's heroine, however, suffers disillusionment and disappointment, as she sacrifices her intellectual and spiritual development for her husband's stillborn project. Readers get the benefit of seeing how Dorothea makes her fateful choices without suffering the pain she endures.

Reading Parables

Every religious tradition has made good use of the parable, which has been defined as "an earthly story with a heavenly meaning." Parables have been described as "narrated metaphors" that encode a particular experience and an abstract category of experiences. They exemplify a highly compressed and concentrated kind of storytelling. With a nod to their value as tools of thinking and learning, James Geary calls them "compact metaphorical thought experiments" (82).

Parables are microcosms, little worlds where important things are condensed in a small space. As Mark Turner has suggested in *The Literary Mind*, in their combination of story and projection—story and meaning—parables offer a paradigm of how we construct meaning in every dimension of our lives (5). Parables embed ideas and project them through a narrative. Moreover, as Michael Wood suggests, parables "require something more than interpretation" (126). Like all forms of literature, parables, Wood contends, cry out to be applied; they invite, when they don't demand, a personal application to our lived experience (127), yet without directing us to any particular uses we might make of them.

Let's consider a familiar parable from the Christian tradition, one of the most famous New Testament parables, the parable of the prodigal son, from the Gospel of Luke, chapter 15.

Here is the beginning of the parable in the King James translation. It is presented a bit at a time, in a "broken" or "interrupted" reading.

A certain man had two sons: and the younger of them said to his father, Father, give me the portion of goods that falleth to me. And he divided unto them his living. And not many days after the younger son gathered all together, and took his journey into a far country, and there wasted his substance with riotous living. And when he had spent all, there arose a mighty famine in that land; and he began to be in want. And he went and joined himself to a citizen of that country; and he sent him into his fields to feed swine. And he would fain have filled his belly with the husks that the swine did eat: and no man gave unto him.

Let's pause here for a moment and make note of a few things—the swiftness of the parable's pace, for example. It doesn't take more than a few sentences to launch the story of the sons, their divided inheritance, and the younger son's squandering of his portion. We might also note how the story conveys the level of desperation to which this prodigal son has sunk—eager to eat the husks of corn fit for pigs. (We won't take the time to do more than note the loathsomeness of swine in Jewish culture in the early years of the first millennium.)

The parable continues:

> And when he came to himself, he said, How many hired servants of my father have bread enough and to spare, and I perish with hunger! I will arise and go to my father, and will say unto him, Father, I have sinned against heaven, and before thee. And am no more worthy to be called thy son: make me as one of thy hired servants. And he arose, and came to his father. But when he was yet a great way off, his father saw him, and had compassion, and ran, and fell on his neck, and kissed him. And the son said unto him, Father, I have sinned against heaven, and in thy sight, and am no more worthy to be called thy son.

This is powerful stuff, owing, in large part, to its language, especially the interior monologue that reflects the son's thoughts as he makes a resolution to return to his father and beg his forgiveness, which we hear twice—once, so to speak in "rehearsal," and then again as the son speaks directly to his father. There is a slight difference between the two little speeches. The actual speech to the father does not include the words that the prodigal son had planned to say: "make me as one of thy hired servants." We might wonder why he omitted those words in speaking to his father.

We can offer a number of possible reasons: (1) because he forgot them; (2) because he decided against saying them—they pushed too far, and he didn't really want to be a servant; (3) because the father interrupted his little speech before he could get that far. But let's ask one other question about this segment of the parable: Is the son sincere in his seeking of forgiveness? Has he really repented? Or is he faking it, only pretending to be sorry for the waste of his

inheritance, and simply trusting to his father's forgiving nature—
"playing" his father, in fact?

Our emphasis so far has been on the dialogue in this part of the
parable. But we should not overlook one of the parable's most
amazing details—a descriptive sentence worth repeating:

> But when he [the son] was yet a great way off, his father saw
> him, and had compassion, and ran, and fell on his neck, and
> kissed him.

How is it that the father saw the son when the son was still a long
way off—except to suggest that the father had been hoping for the
son's return, waiting, even looking out to the horizon for him? And
that word "compassion" is fraught with feeling. The father's emotion cannot be held in check—he just can't wait for his son to come
to him. Instead, he runs to his son, puts his arms around him (falls
on his neck)—you can't get any closer to someone physically—and
kisses him. Every one of those verbs ("ran," "fell," and "kissed")
suggests the intensity of the father's feelings, the depth of his love
for his prodigal son.

So it's not just the details of speech—the dialogue—that matter
here. Details of description and action assume great significance.

Here's the next part of the story:

> But the father said to his servants, Bring forth the best
> robe, and put it on him, and put a ring on his hand, and
> shoes on his feet. And bring hither the fatted calf, and kill
> it, and let us eat, and be merry: For this my son was dead,
> and is alive again; he was lost, and is found. And they began
> to be merry.

That initial "but" is important, indicating a shift, as the father
shifts from what the son is saying—that he's not worthy—to what
the father wants to do. The father does not respond directly to
what the son has said. He ignores it, pretends that he hasn't heard
it. Instead of responding directly to his son, the father responds
indirectly—by commanding the servants to kill the fatted calf—and

not just any calf, but a choice one ready for the fire. We notice, of course, as well, how the father wants the best robe and shoes and a ring for his son—signs of favor and kinship and honor.

One last note about this section: that wonderful image the father uses—the metaphor of the son's return to life (he was dead and is alive again), the son's being found after he had been lost. One of those metaphorical shifts occurs in two other parables in Luke, chapter 15, along with the parable of the prodigal son. The other parables are shorter and simpler and describe only what was lost being found. They set up and prepare for the more complex rendering of this parable's teaching and its deeper metaphor about life and death.

But let us move now to the parable's final section. There's trouble brewing, if you recall, in the mind and heart of an elder brother:

> Now his elder son was in the field: and as he came and drew nigh to the house, he heard music and dancing. And he called one of the servants, and asked what these things meant. And he said unto him, Thy brother is come; and thy father hath killed the fatted calf, because he hath received him safe and sound. And he was angry, and would not go in: therefore came his father out, and entreated him. And he answering said to his father, "Lo, these many years do I serve thee, neither transgressed I at any time thy commandment, and yet thou never gavest me a kid, that I might make merry with my friends: But as soon as this thy son was come, which hath devoured thy living with harlots, thou hast killed for him the fatted calf. And he said unto him, Son, thou art ever with me, and all that I have is thine. It was meet that we should make merry, and be glad: for this thy brother was dead, and is alive again: and was lost, and is found.

How does the elder brother discover what's happening? He hears music and dancing and wonders what's going on. Imagine his surprise—or more likely his shock and indignation—when the servants tell him the cause of the celebration. He refuses to participate in the festivities, and instead launches into a speech in which there is a strong jibe at his brother: the brother whom he never calls "brother"—only his father's son—the son "which hath devoured thy living with harlots," that son, so different from him, the older faithful son, who never violated his father's trust, who was always there for his father, the faithful son for whom the father never held such a celebration.

At this point, we can raise the question of fairness. It doesn't seem fair; it's just not right. Or is it? It depends, of course, on context and perspective. From a human standpoint—from a secular perspective—the elder son has a legitimate complaint. It isn't fair. It's unjust to reward the wasteful squandering son and to take for granted the loyal one. But from a Christian perspective, it makes sense. The parable of the prodigal son offers an illustration, an example, of how much the heavenly father loves humankind, even when people behave like the prodigal son—as long as they repent and seek forgiveness. So the parable is a metaphor for God the Father's love. And whether we read it as a Christian parable about God's love, or as a metaphor for the love of human fathers for their wayward sons (or daughters), the parable serves as a powerful provocation to thinking about a host of inescapable issues—about the mutual relations and responsibilities of fathers and sons (and, by extension, of parents and children), about error and failure, about recognition and repentance, about fairness, about forgiveness, about justice, about mercy, about love.

Two Zen Parables

Parables from other spiritual traditions provide similar rewards for careful readers. Compelling examples can be found in Judaism, Islam, Confucianism, Taoism, Hinduism, and Jainism, among the world's major religious traditions. Two Zen parables I find especially interesting are "Learning to Be Silent" and "Muddy Road." Both appear in *Zen Flesh, Zen Bones*, compiled by Paul Reps, which also contains an ample selection of Zen koans.

Because parables omit explicit morals like those of fables, it's up to readers to determine the lessons a parable teaches. To stretch our interpretive abilities, it's useful to identify multiple morals for a parable and perhaps to imagine a title for each of the morals or lessons we extract from it.

Here is the first of these provocative Zen parables:

Learning to Be Silent

The pupils of the Tendai school used to study meditation before Zen entered Japan. Four of them who were intimate friends promised one another to observe seven days of silence.

On the first day all were silent. Their meditation had begun auspiciously, but when night came and the oil lamps were growing dim, one of the pupils could not help exclaiming to a servant: "Fix those lamps."

The second pupil was surprised to hear the first one talk: "We are not supposed to say a word," he remarked.

"You two are stupid. Why did you talk?" asked the third.

"I am the only one who has not talked," concluded the fourth pupil.

COMMENTS

Part of our pleasure in reading and hearing such a story—for this is very much a spoken story, one told as part of an oral tradition—derives from the way its action unfolds and its characters behave. We can enjoy the crispness of the story's dialogue and the different ways each friend violates the promise to keep silent. We can also admire how the author or teller paces the narrative—how, as in a well-told joke, we sense a buildup toward a deftly delivered punch line. With observations like these, we are attending to the story's creative aspects.

Once we have had some time to think about the parable, and read it a few times, we can consider its focus and central concerns. What is this story about? What is its main concept—its essential idea and teaching? What truths does the story suggest? Is the story primarily about silence—perhaps about the difficulty of keeping silent for any length of time? If so, why might "silence" be an important goal—for whom, under what circumstances, and with what purpose(s)? Or do we think the story is concerned more with the larger issue of "self-control," the discipline of monitoring one's behavior? And if this is our primary (though not exclusive) sense of it, why might the idea of discipline or self-control be important? Toward what end are discipline and self-control directed?

In fact, if we think of "silence" as the central issue, we can consider the purpose of maintaining silence, which leads, perhaps, to notions of discipline and self-control. The questions we ask about these concepts are the same ones to ask about silence—discipline or self-control for what purpose, toward what goal?

But perhaps we think the story isn't really about silence or discipline primarily, but rather about vanity and competition, about people's desire to outperform others, about their desire to succeed where others fail, and to boast about it and lord it over them. Perhaps we have other ideas. Clearly, there is more than one lesson embedded in and suggested by "Learning to Be Silent."

In raising this series of possible ways to think about "Learning to Be Silent," we have been trying on different perspectives. In the process, we have been considering different interpretations, as we entertain various alternatives and possibilities. In a way, we have been doing exactly this while considering different emphases in our discussion of the parable.

We can think about and "see" a story not just in different ways—from multiple perspectives—but also from opposite perspectives, from contrasting points of view. In thinking about the pupils in "Learning to Be Silent," we noticed that each of them failed to keep the promise to be silent. We might add, too, that they failed pretty quickly. Their goal was a week of silence, but they couldn't even make it through one full day. As a result, our interpretation of the story—and the moral or lesson drawn from it—might very well reflect this significant failure.

On the other hand, however, we can consider the story from an opposite perspective. By putting a positive spin on its outcome, we can entertain an alternative explanation. Can you, for the sake of argument, see the pupils' failure as somehow "good" for them? Can you extract something beneficial for them from their experience?

Suppose, for example, we argue that the friends learned just how hard it is to achieve silence, an important lesson. Let's remember that they are students (the word "pupils" occurs four times), and that they have only just begun the long journey toward a mastery of silence. We might, then, give them credit for choosing an ambitious goal and for making it silently through part of the day—the daylight part, even though they broke their silence when darkness came on. They have made a start—a bit of progress—haven't they, toward achieving a challenging goal?

Even in a very brief narrative like "Learning to Be Silent," we can make other shifts of perspective and attention. We can ask ourselves, for example, about the keeper(s) of the lamps. Who are the servants in the story? What is their role? Why don't they speak? Does it matter? Why does one of the students use a peremptory tone—and in what other possible ways might he have voiced his concern and his need with regard to the dimming of the lamps? How, in short, does he treat the silent and invisible servant? What might we make of that treatment?

Another direction we might take with our thinking is toward the story's setting. Where does it take place? And when? How do we know? On what basis do we make our inferences about the time and place of its action? We might also ask why those details are not more fully specified in the story. The strategy here, then, is to consider what is unspoken and unsaid, to notice, paradoxically, what is missing, what is omitted rather than included.

We might also ask why such a story would be told in the first place—and by whom. This kind of question leads us to considerations of context—conditions outside the story's text and details. For "Learning to Be Silent," it is important to consider the context of genre—the kind of story it is—and also the context of religion, since it's a Zen parable. Since "Learning to Be Silent" comes from the Zen Buddhist religious tradition, we can expect that one of its central lessons will reflect important Zen teachings. One of those teachings involves the importance of silence because silence is necessary for meditation, and meditation is the way to achieve an inner stillness, which, in turn, is necessary to arrive at the state of *satori*, or enlightenment. Zen puts great emphasis on the need for the mind to control the body—to shut out its insistent distractions so that inner peace can be found and enlightenment achieved. Thus silence is essential for successful meditation, which is required to achieve the essential and central goal—to reach a state of enlightenment, the kind of spiritual experience sought by Buddhists, especially by adherents of Zen Buddhism.

These contextual aspects of "Learning to Be Silent" enrich our understanding and deepen our appreciation of the parable. Even if we lack knowledge of its genre and context, however, we can still enjoy it. We can think about the important lessons it teaches, though our emphasis, without contextual understanding, is likely to be more secular than religious.

And now here is an additional Zen parable for your consideration:

Muddy Road

Tanzan and Ekido were once traveling together down a muddy road. A heavy rain was still falling. Coming around a bend, they met a lovely girl in a silk kimono and sash, unable to cross the intersection.

"Come on, girl," said Tanzan at once. Lifting her in his arms, he carried her over the mud.

Ekido did not speak again until that night, when they reached a lodging temple. Then he no longer could restrain himself. "We monks don't go near females," he told Tanzan, "especially not young and lovely ones. It is dangerous. Why did you do that?"

"I left the girl there," said Tanzan. "Are you still carrying her?"

Like "Learning to Be Silent," "Muddy Road" turns on the issue of speech and silence. And it turns, even more importantly, on the notion of what it means to "carry" someone, and to carry various kinds of burdens. Tanzan's act of carrying the girl over the mud is swiftly executed and as quickly forgotten. Ekido's "carrying" of

Tanzan's action is much more pronounced and far more prolonged. Ekido bears a far heavier metaphorical weight—until his burden becomes too much for him, and he blurts out his remark to Tanzan in frustrated anger. Tanzan's retort is as swift and decisive as his action: "I left the girl there," he says. "Are you still carrying her?" Tanzan's rebuke of Ekido hits him and us with the characteristic sudden jolt of Zen understanding.

We might also consider the implications of Ekido's words and of Tanzan's response. We could reflect on the difference between the spirit and the letter of the proscriptions invoked. And we might want to make connections between the two parables, and between them and parables from other religious traditions. We can derive considerable pleasure from reading parables, both those from traditions familiar to us and those from traditions we know less about.

Fiction and Reality

Fiction differs from history in being factually untrue. Literature in general and fiction, specifically, deal in universal truths, not in particular truths. As Northrop Frye points out in *The Educated Imagination*, we become interested in Achilles not because there was a particular individual named Achilles, but because Achilles represents something we admire and fear, something we might aspire to be or wish to avoid becoming (65). Achilles performs the feats of great warriors. His anger and resentment, his wrath and heroism reflect aspects of ourselves. In reading about his and other heroes' exploits in Homer's *Iliad*, we are not reading about what actually happened, but about the kinds of things that generally happen in war. Homer provides not the specific but the typical. He presents those typical actions and events, describes those typical feats by identifying individual characters—Achilles, Ajax, Agamemnon, among them—who perform those deeds.

When we read a work of fiction, we re-create in our imagination what the writer has created in words. The writer's fictional world is related to the actual world, but differs from it in being conjured up in and through language. Sven Birkerts, in *Reading Life*, describes this literary legerdemain as the "power to compel belief in a reality that differs from the known" (17).

Analogous to Birkerts's suggestion, George Eliot, in "The Natural History of German Life," writes: "Art [including, of course, literature] is the nearest thing to life; it is a mode of amplifying our experience and extending our contact with our fellow men beyond the bounds of our personal lot" (cited in Wood, *Nearest* 110). And Wendy Lesser suggests in *Why I Read* that fiction takes us to an "elsewhere made accessible to [us] through the efforts of another imagination, collaborating for a time with [y]our own" (146). Art imitates life, but does not replicate or replace it; art, in fact, is part of life.

Yet the appeal to us as readers of novels and stories is less their verisimilitude, or true-to-life-likeness—the degree to which they imitate the world as we know it—and more how fiction echoes the real world while remaining separate from it. Herman Melville puts it like this in *The Confidence Man*: "It is with fiction as with religion: it should present another world, but one to which we feel the tie" (216).

Literature and Knowledge

Following the lead of Michael Wood in *Literature and the Taste of Knowledge*, I consider next the kinds of knowledge literature affords us. "What does literature know?" is Wood's provocative question. His somewhat abstract answer is that it includes the "gap between knowledge and life, between what can be said and can't" (11). For Wood, literature's knowledge is conveyed obliquely (9), yet surely. A more specific answer, I suggest, is that literature knows how people live and think; it knows how they act, and it surmises why they act as they do. Literature understands that human beings err, that they undermine their better nature, sabotage their nobler impulses, lie to themselves, trick themselves, sometimes self-destruct. Literature presents this kind of knowledge, this understanding of human behavior, with psychological acuity and social understanding in the form of drama and action, of plot and character relationships, of language and form. It does so through suggestion, through implication rather than direct explanation.

One of the paradoxes of the relationship between literature and knowledge is that literary works include affirmations and outright instructions—admonitions, recommendations, guidance in how to act—even while they need to be read inferentially and interpretively, rather than as explicitly admonitory. Wood contends that a literary work's affirmations are genuine, even when we might wish to argue against them, and even though they are presented "as if," in a fictive creation (101–103).

Some examples: W. H. Auden's "About suffering they were never wrong / The Old Masters," from his "Musée des Beaux Arts." And Theodore Roethke's "I learn by going where I have to go," from "The Waking." Also Leo Tolstoy's "All happy families are alike; all unhappy families are unhappy in their own way," the opening sentence of *Anna Karenina*. Such affirmations are genuine in that they play a role in the work of which they are a part. Even so, however, readers can strip them of their context, seeing them as propositions that illustrate or otherwise reflect some truth about human experience—some philosophical notion, psychological aperçu, or sociological theory. However, because these propositions are part of an imagined world in a fictive work, we accept them as having a kind of double life. On one hand, they exist as matters of fact, within their fictive worlds. On the other, they transcend their literary environments to comment on and convey advice about our human lives outside of literature.

So too with the guidance or instruction a work might seem to provide, as for example, Rainer Maria Rilke's advice in "Archaic Torso of Apollo": "You must change your life." Wood contends that an instruction like this is oblique not merely because it's arguable, but also because such admonitions ask a great deal of us without providing guidance in how and where we might begin to implement them (105). In response to Rilke's speaker, we might ask, How should we change our lives? Where should we begin? And, we can ask ourselves more generally how we can respond to such counsels, what they might mean for us in practice.

These examples are from poetry, and so we might consider, as well, what kinds of knowledge fiction, especially the novel, provides. One answer, of course, is that fiction provides knowledge of society and of individuals finding their place (or not) in that society. Novels oscillate between individual and social emphases, the best of them (the most important and influential examples) negotiating the multiple tensions and ambiguities embodied in individuals finding their place in, beyond, or against the social worlds they inhabit. Think, for example, of *Wuthering Heights*, *The Mill on the Floss*, *Little Dorrit*, *Tess of the D'Urbervilles*, *Vanity Fair*, *Portrait of a Lady*, *The Awakening*, *To the Lighthouse*, *The Great Gatsby*, *The Sound and the Fury*, *A Farewell to Arms*, *Invisible Man*, *The House of the Spirits*, *Beloved*, and *The Handmaid's Tale*, among scores of others.

Novels also provide us with psychological understanding; the most penetrating of them yield insights into patterns of thought, including decision making, delusional thinking, erroneous inference making, and other forms of mistaken ideas and misunderstandings. Novels also lead us toward a knowledge of consciousness, which has its roots in nineteenth-century works such as *Middlemarch* and *Crime and Punishment*, but which becomes more complex in later works, such as *Ulysses* and *Mrs. Dalloway*. We can learn a great deal about psychology and sociology from reading novels like these, as they offer us ways to understand the mysteries of human character and the complexities of social relationships.

Psychological insights gleaned from the great nineteenth-century Brazilian, English, French, German, Russian, and other nations' novels also butt up against social, political, cultural, and economic realities. Once fiction abandons realism, however, it provides less a knowledge of society and of psychological states than of language itself and of philosophical and political impulses and instigations. These observations, of course, represent broad strokes, and can only highlight some of the ways fiction conveys knowledge, deepens readers' understanding of themselves and of the world: forms of knowing valuable for living. Let us look briefly at two notable examples of what a novel knows, Herman Melville's *Moby-Dick* and Virginia Woolf's *To the Lighthouse*.

Moby-Dick *and* To the Lighthouse

To some extent, Melville's book is an exploration of knowing, what can and cannot be known; it's an epistemological work, a search for knowledge and meaning. Its narrator, Ishmael, who waxes and wanes as a narrative voice and presence, is bookish and philosophical; he wants to "see" the world so as to understand it, to discover the significance of what he experiences. He is like Ahab in his compulsion to know, but differs from Ahab in what he yearns to know. Ishmael seeks to understand the whale as a creature, but he can't decide just what a whale is, essentially. Though he attempts to define and classify the whale, he has trouble deciding with any degree of confidence even what its spout vapor and skin consist of. In various ways—through the science of cetology, the art of painting, and the limitations of language—the task of representing the reality and mystery of Leviathan is shown to be impossible.

To Ahab, the white whale represents a mask behind which lies the explanation of its mystery. The whale is a natural phenomenon that walls off and inhibits understanding. For Ahab, the creature is an obstacle to understanding, to penetrating the mystery of existence. Thus he vows to continue his quest to strike through the mask, the wall of appearance, even if only to discover that there is nothing behind or beyond it.

What Melville shows repeatedly throughout *Moby-Dick* is the limitation of human knowledge—how full comprehension is impossible, the whale being an ungraspable phantom in terms of what can be known of its essential nature, while, ironically, it is captured and dismembered and put to myriad human uses. Even so, Moby-Dick the individual whale and Moby-Dick the symbol remain perennially and perpetually mysterious and ultimately unknowable. This knowledge *Moby-Dick*, the book, offers us.

If Melville's novel says anything about literature and knowledge, it suggests that satisfactory conclusions are scarce as hens' teeth, to appropriate Melville's simile for finding whales in the vastness of the ocean. It suggests that final, definitive explanations of natural forces are not possible. All we are left with is the insatiable human mind and its ultimately unsatisfiable quest for knowledge. Driven by their radically different impulses toward knowledge, Ahab and Ishmael discover the impossibility of penetrating the mystery, hampered by the ineluctable limitations of human understanding.

Virginia Woolf's *To the Lighthouse* takes a different tack. Through a rigorously restricted rendering of internal thought and experience, Woolf portrays human consciousness in all its associational subjectivity. She explores character from the inside, through mental association, representing the mind in the act of thinking. She depicts the flow of thought, the stream of consciousness, revealing her characters' varied states of mind and the diverse forms of thinking they exhibit. This is a different kind of knowledge from that of *Moby-Dick*, a type of knowledge anticipated in the nineteenth century by George Eliot in novels like *Middlemarch*, especially. Eliot's novel, however, evokes a character's inner thought *externally*, through the device of omniscient narration, at which she excelled. Its originator, Montaigne, in his *Essais*, represented his own mind, rather than the minds of fictional characters, as Eliot does. Montaigne analyzed his mind in constant motion, charting its fluctuations, as he portrayed his idiosyncrasies and peculiarities in all their unique particularity. The first stream-of-consciousness writer, Montaigne was admired by Woolf, who composed an appreciative essay about him, while writing her more minutely determined stream-of-consciousness fiction, in which she portrays minds in the immediacy of minute-by-minute associational movement.

Woolf's fiction reveals the power and influence of memory on the human mind. The truths of experience that Woolf's novels capture, *Mrs. Dalloway* and *To the Lighthouse*, especially, rely on the memories we can't escape, memories that bring past and present into coinciding existence, as when Woolf shows a character like Lily Briscoe experiencing multiple moments simultaneously. Paradoxically, moments of time are both connected and fragmented; split off from their historical context, moments of past time coexist with later present moments for Woolf as "moments of being."

Woolf presents her characters' inner thoughts and feelings by means of an internal monologue we are permitted to overhear. She takes us inside her characters' minds, where their thoughts and feelings, ideas and attitudes, mix and mingle, merge and separate as they come in and out of focus, involuntarily. In reading *To the Lighthouse*, we come to understand the constant flux of the mind; we experience its unstructured, shifting, impressionistic nature, as Woolf captures the felt sense of the innermost rhythms of consciousness.

If Melville conveys the limitations of human knowledge through the contrasting perspectives and actions, mental and physical, of Ishmael and Ahab, Woolf conveys the contrasting states of mind of Mr. and Mrs. Ramsay, with Mrs. Ramsay possessing a knowledge from within, intuitively, and Mr. Ramsay knowledge from without, logically. Their pursuit of knowledge and their experience of knowing are both contradictory and complementary. Mr. Ramsay seeks order and precision; his mind knows things sequentially and linearly. Mrs. Ramsay, by contrast, seeks unity and completeness; her holistic knowledge is possible in singular moments of vision and of being. It becomes increasingly clear which of these ways of knowing Woolf favors, as Mrs. Ramsay embodies and enacts virtues and values *To the Lighthouse* celebrates. Woolf centers the novel on her. It is her presence and her influence on the book's other characters that move its plot and establish its character relations. It is her aura that the book evokes and captures in all its mysterious beauty.

Joyce's "The Boarding House" and the Elements of Fiction

Yet another way into a writer's accomplishment in a story is to consider how it deploys the elements of fiction. Any of the stories from James Joyce's *Dubliners* might be profitably analyzed this way. I have chosen a little masterpiece, "The Boarding House," to reprint here, followed by a discussion of the story's plot and structure, character and characterization, setting, point of view, tone, and thematic implications.

The Boarding House

Mrs. Mooney was a butcher's daughter. She was a woman who was quite able to keep things to herself: a determined woman. She had married her father's foreman and opened a butcher's shop near Spring Gardens. But as soon as his father-in-law was dead Mr. Mooney began to go to the devil. He drank, plundered the till, ran headlong into debt. It was no use making him take the pledge: he was sure to break out again a few days after. By fighting his wife in the presence of customers and by buying bad meat he ruined his business. One night he went for his wife with the cleaver and she had to sleep at a neighbour's house.

After that they lived apart. She went to the priest and got a separation from him with care of the children. She would give him neither money nor food nor house-room; and so he was obliged to enlist himself as a sheriff's man. He was a shabby stooped little drunkard with a white face and a white moustache and white eyebrows, pencilled above his little eyes, which were veined and raw; and all day long he sat in the bailiff's room, waiting to be put on a job. Mrs. Mooney, who had taken what remained of her money out of the butcher business and set up a boarding house in Hardwicke Street, was a big imposing woman. Her house had a floating population made up of tourists from Liverpool and the Isle of Man and, occasionally, artistes from the music halls. Its resident population was made up of clerks from the city. She governed the house cunningly and firmly, knew when to give credit, when to be stern and when to let things pass. All the resident young men spoke of her as *The Madam*.

Mrs. Mooney's young men paid fifteen shillings a week for board and lodgings (beer or stout at dinner excluded). They shared in common tastes and occupations and for this reason they were very chummy with one another. They discussed with one another the chances of favourites and outsiders. Jack Mooney, the Madam's son, who was clerk to a commission agent in Fleet Street, had the reputation of being a hard case. He was fond of using soldiers' obscenities: usually he came home in the small hours. When he met his friends he had always a good one to tell them and he was always sure to be on to a good thing—that is to say, a likely horse or a likely *artiste*. He was also handy with the mits and sang comic songs. On Sunday nights there would often be a reunion in Mrs. Mooney's front drawing-room. The music-hall *artistes* would oblige; and Sheridan played waltzes and polkas and vamped accompaniments. Polly Mooney, the Madam's daughter, would also sing. She sang:

> *I'm a . . . naughty girl.*
> *You needn't sham:*
> *You know I am.*

Polly was a slim girl of nineteen; she had light soft hair and a small full mouth. Her eyes, which were grey with a shade of green through them, had a habit of glancing upwards when she spoke with anyone, which made her look like a little perverse madonna. Mrs. Mooney had first sent her daughter to be a typist in a corn-factor's office but, as a disreputable sheriff's man used to come every other day to the office, asking to be allowed to say a word to his daughter, she had taken her daughter home again and set her to do housework. As Polly was very lively the intention was to give her the run of the young men. Besides young men like to feel that there is a young woman not very far away. Polly, of course, flirted with the young men but Mrs. Mooney, who was a shrewd judge, knew that the young men were only passing the time away: none of them meant business. Things went on so for a long time and Mrs. Mooney began to think of sending Polly back to typewriting when she noticed that something was going on between Polly and one of the young men. She watched the pair and kept her own counsel.

Polly knew that she was being watched, but still her mother's persistent silence could not be misunderstood. There had been no open complicity between mother and daughter, no open understanding but, though people in the house began to talk of the affair, still Mrs. Mooney did not intervene. Polly began to grow a little strange in her manner and the young man was evidently perturbed. At last, when she judged it to be the right moment, Mrs. Mooney intervened. She dealt with moral problems as a cleaver deals with meat: and in this case she had made up her mind.

It was a bright Sunday morning of early summer, promising heat, but with a fresh breeze blowing. All the windows of the boarding house were open and the lace curtains ballooned gently towards the street beneath the raised sashes. The belfry of George's Church sent out constant peals and worshippers, singly or in groups, traversed the little circus before the church, revealing their purpose by their self-contained demeanour no less than by the little volumes in their gloved hands. Breakfast was over in the boarding house and the table of the breakfast-room was covered with plates on which lay yellow streaks of eggs with morsels of bacon-fat and bacon-rind. Mrs. Mooney sat in the straw arm-chair and watched the servant Mary remove the breakfast things. She made Mary collect the crusts and pieces of broken bread to help to make Tuesday's bread-pudding. When the table was cleared, the broken bread collected, the sugar and butter safe under lock and key, she began to reconstruct the interview which she had had the night before with Polly. Things were as she had suspected: she had been frank in her questions and Polly had been frank in her answers. Both had been somewhat awkward, of course. She had been made awkward by her not wishing to receive the news in too cavalier a fashion or to seem to have connived and Polly had been made awkward not merely because allusions of that kind always made her awkward but also because she did not wish it to be thought that in her wise innocence she had divined the intention behind her mother's tolerance.

Mrs. Mooney glanced instinctively at the little gilt clock on the mantelpiece as soon as she had become aware through her revery that the bells of George's Church had stopped ringing. It was seventeen minutes past eleven: she would have lots of time to have the matter out with Mr. Doran and then catch short twelve at Marlborough Street. She was sure she would win. To begin with she had all the weight of social opinion on her side: she was an outraged mother. She had allowed him to live beneath her roof, assuming that he was a man of honour and he had simply abused her hospitality. He was thirty-four or thirty-five years of age, so that youth could not be pleaded as his excuse; nor could ignorance be his excuse since he was a man who had seen something of the world. He had simply taken advantage of Polly's youth and inexperience: that was evident. The question was: What reparation would he make?

There must be reparation made in such case. It is all very well for the man: he can go his ways as if nothing had happened, having had his moment of pleasure, but the girl has to bear the brunt. Some mothers would be content to patch up such an affair for a sum of money; she had known cases of it. But she would not do so. For her only one reparation could make up for the loss of her daughter's honour: marriage.

She counted all her cards again before sending Mary up to Doran's room to say that she wished to speak with him. She felt sure she would win. He was a serious young man, not rakish or loud-voiced like the others. If it had been Mr. Sheridan or Mr. Meade or Bantam Lyons her task would have been much harder. She did not think he would face publicity. All the lodgers in the house knew something of the affair; details had been invented by some. Besides, he had been employed for thirteen years in a great Catholic wine-merchant's office and publicity would mean for him, perhaps, the loss of his job. Whereas if he agreed all might be well. She knew he had a good screw for one thing and she suspected he had a bit of stuff put by.

Nearly the half-hour! She stood up and surveyed herself in the pier-glass. The decisive expression of her great florid face satisfied her and she thought of some mothers she knew who could not get their daughters off their hands.

Mr. Doran was very anxious indeed this Sunday morning. He had made two attempts to shave but his hand had been so unsteady that he had been obliged to desist. Three days' reddish beard fringed his jaws and every two or three minutes a mist gathered on his glasses so that he had to take them off and polish them with his pocket-handkerchief. The recollection of his confession of the night before was a cause of acute pain to him; the priest had drawn out every ridiculous detail of the affair and in the end had so magnified his sin that he was almost thankful at being afforded a loophole of reparation. The harm was done. What could he do now but marry her or run away? He could not brazen it out. The affair would be sure to be talked of and his employer would be certain to hear of it. Dublin is such a small city: everyone knows everyone else's business. He felt his heart leap warmly in his throat as he heard in his excited imagination old Mr. Leonard calling out in his rasping voice: "Send Mr. Doran here, please."

All his long years of service gone for nothing! All his industry and diligence thrown away! As a young man he had sown his wild oats, of course; he had boasted of his freethinking and denied the existence of God to his companions in public-houses. But that was all passed and done with . . . nearly. He still bought a copy of *Reynolds's Newspaper* every week but he attended to his religious duties and for nine-tenths of the year lived a regular life. He had money enough to settle down on; it was not that. But the family would look down on her. First of all there was her disreputable father and then her mother's boarding house was beginning to get a certain fame. He had a notion that he was being had. He could imagine his friends talking of the affair and laughing. She *was* a little vulgar; some times she said "I seen" and "If I had've known." But what would grammar matter if he really loved her? He could not make up his mind whether to like her or despise her for what she had done. Of course he had done it too. His instinct urged him to remain free, not to marry. Once you are married you are done for, it said.

While he was sitting helplessly on the side of the bed in shirt and trousers she tapped lightly at his door and entered.

She told him all, that she had made a clean breast of it to her mother and that her mother would speak with him that morning. She cried and threw her arms round his neck, saying:

"O Bob! Bob! What am I to do? What am I to do at all?"

She would put an end to herself, she said.

He comforted her feebly, telling her not to cry, that it would be all right, never fear. He felt against his shirt the agitation of her bosom.

It was not altogether his fault that it had happened. He remembered well, with the curious patient memory of the celibate, the first casual caresses her dress, her breath, her fingers had given him. Then late one night as he was undressing for bed she had tapped at his door, timidly. She wanted to relight her candle at his for hers had been blown out by a gust. It was her bath night. She wore a loose open combing-jacket of printed flannel. Her white instep shone in the opening of her furry slippers and the blood glowed warmly behind her perfumed skin. From her hands and wrists too as she lit and steadied her candle a faint perfume arose.

On nights when he came in very late it was she who warmed up his dinner. He scarcely knew what he was eating feeling her beside him alone, at night, in the sleeping house. And her thoughtfulness! If the night was anyway cold or wet or windy there was sure to be a little tumbler of punch ready for him. Perhaps they could be happy together. . . . They used to go upstairs together on tiptoe, each with a candle, and on the third landing exchange reluctant goodnights. They used to kiss. He remembered well her eyes, the touch of her hand and his delirium. . . .

But delirium passes. He echoed her phrase, applying it to himself: "*What am I to do?*" The instinct of the celibate warned him to hold back. But the sin was there; even his sense of honour told him that reparation must be made for such a sin.

While he was sitting with her on the side of the bed Mary came to the door and said that the missus wanted to see him in the parlour. He stood up to put on his coat and waistcoat, more helpless than ever. When he was dressed he went over to her to comfort her. It would be all right, never fear. He left her crying on the bed and moaning softly: "*O my God!*"

Going down the stairs his glasses became so dimmed with moisture that he had to take them off and polish them. He longed to ascend through the roof and fly away to another country where he would never hear again of his trouble, and yet a force pushed him downstairs step by step. The implacable faces of his employer and of the Madam stared upon his discomfiture. On the last flight of stairs he passed Jack Mooney who was coming up from the pantry nursing two bottles of *Bass*. They saluted coldly; and the lover's eyes rested for a second or two on a thick bulldog face and a pair of thick short arms. When he reached the foot of the staircase he glanced up and saw Jack regarding him from the door of the return-room.

Suddenly he remembered the night when one of the music hall *artistes*, a little blond Londoner, had made a rather free allusion to Polly. The reunion had been almost broken up on account of Jack's violence. Everyone tried to quiet him. The music-hall *artiste*, a little paler than usual, kept smiling and saying that there was no harm meant: but Jack kept shouting at him that if any fellow tried that sort of a game on with *his* sister he'd bloody well put his teeth down his throat, so he would.

Polly sat for a little time on the side of the bed, crying. Then she dried her eyes and went over to the looking-glass. She dipped the end of the towel in the water-jug and refreshed her eyes with the cool water. She looked at herself in profile and readjusted a hairpin above her ear. Then she went back to the bed again and sat at the foot. She regarded the pillows for a long time and the sight of them awakened in her mind secret, amiable memories. She rested the nape of her neck against the cool iron bed-rail and fell into a reverie. There was no longer any perturbation visible on her face.

She waited on patiently, almost cheerfully, without alarm, her memories gradually giving place to hopes and visions of the future. Her hopes and visions were so intricate that she no longer saw the white pillows on which her gaze was fixed or remembered that she was waiting for anything.

At last she heard her mother calling. She started to her feet and ran to the banisters.

"Polly! Polly!"

"Yes, mamma?"

"Come down, dear. Mr. Doran wants to speak to you."

Then she remembered what she had been waiting for.

COMMENTS

Plot and Structure

What can we say about the plot of "The Boarding House?" What might we emphasize about the story's action, and about its shape as a structured artifact? In terms of its plot, or developing action, I would highlight how the story moves quickly from a focus on Mrs. Mooney to a close look at her daughter, Polly, who makes her appearance at the end of the third paragraph and dominates the story from there, though sharing the spotlight with Bob Doran, until returning, triumphantly, to Mrs. Mooney at the end. Polly's sexual allure is emphasized such that readers suspect that something will happen as a result, given a boarding house populated by young men. Mrs. Mooney appears inactive during Polly's seduction of Bob Doran, with his decent job and middle-class respectability, such that Mrs. Mooney's hovering in the margins of the story's action is a deliberate ploy, an invitation, even a form of encouragement to Polly to work her wiles on the unsuspecting, eagerly complicit Doran. Plot, in this story, includes the collusion between mother and daughter to entrap an eligible marriage prospect.

The plot centers on and advances Doran's decision to marry Polly; and it turns, as well, on Mrs. Mooney's decision to delay her confrontation with Mr. Doran, thereby intensifying his sense of foreboding and diminishing his chance of escape. Joyce withholds from us the actual scene of sexual seduction, Doran's and Polly's intimacy having occurred before the story's action begins. Joyce provides us with a flashback midway through the story from Doran's perspective. Even that scene is brief and rendered through Doran's memory, revealing his anguished confusion.

Structurally, the story begins and ends with Mrs. Mooney in firm control, first of her boarding house, and then of Polly's and Doran's predicament. In terms of structure, as well, we should consider why the story ends where and as it does, with Doran and Mrs. Mooney waiting in the parlor for Polly to come downstairs. Why does Joyce withhold from us the conversation that surely ensues? What do we imagine of Polly and Doran's future? Joyce leaves these later imaginings to us, as he also leaves us to imagine the particulars of Mrs. Mooney's interrogation of Doran, what they said to one another, how they conducted themselves, what they felt and thought during their private meeting in the parlor, Polly waiting upstairs expectantly.

Character and Characterization

What's particularly interesting in terms of character in "The Boarding House" is how Joyce depicts each of its major figures. He introduces Mrs. Mooney in the story's opening words by means of factual information (she was a butcher's daughter) accompanied by judgment (she keeps things to herself, she is determined, and she can run a business). A butcher's daughter, she does not stand high on the social ladder, her status worsened by her husband's alcoholism, which ruins their business. Undeterred by this failure, however, Mrs. Mooney opens a boarding house and runs it "cunningly and firmly," showing herself to be a "shrewd judge" of character.

For these qualities we may grant Mrs. Mooney a measure of respect. And yet our admiration for her does not lack qualification, as we learn that she is referred to as "the Madam," with its tinge of moral disrepute. Moral dubiety attaches to her, as we see how she uses Polly as bait to attract young male boarders to her residence, allowing Polly to flirt with them in hopes of finding one who might "mean business," business of course meaning marriage.

Polly, as Joyce characterizes her, is a little temptress, whose charms derive in part from her forwardness ("*I'm a . . . naughty girl*," she teases), and in part from her pretense of being shy and a bit reclusive. Joyce writes that "her eyes . . . had a habit of glancing upwards when she spoke with anyone, which made her look like a little perverse madonna." Her slimness suggests vulnerability, while her full mouth hints at sensuality. Her association with the Madonna, the Virgin Mary (perversely), is suggested rather than stated outright; it nicely balances her mother's designation as a "Madam," which is also hinted at—both are left to the reader's imagination, as they are left to the imagination of the boarders at Mrs. Mooney's establishment.

Joyce uses two additional devices of characterization in this story: he reveals a character's state of mind through surface details, such as the fogging of Bob Doran's glasses and the way his hand shakes while he attempts unsuccessfully to shave. He also reveals characters by letting us enter their consciousness, telling us what they think and feel. There is no confusion about who is in command in this miniature family drama. The story ends with Polly's answering her mother's call—an action that confirms Mrs. Mooney as its leading actor and controlling presence. Like Polly, Mr. Doran follows the orders of his future mother-in-law.

Setting

Setting in the *Dubliners* stories, "The Boarding House" included, is essential to meaning. The Catholicism of Bob Doran and of Mrs. Mooney influences their behavior. Doran believes that he needs to make "reparation" for his sexual sin by marrying Polly, his guilty conscience rooted in his Catholic cultural heritage. Mrs. Mooney is determined to use his guilt as leverage, which, however, results less from her Catholic beliefs than from a strategic bit of psychological jujitsu, turning Doran's faith and her understanding of what that faith entails into a means to manipulate him.

That's one way Catholicism is embedded in "The Boarding House." Another is in a series of references to outward manifestations of form—as, for example, that Mrs. Mooney looks to attend a short Sunday mass so that she will have enough time to engage with Mr. Doran in a serious talk and let him know what is required of him. Doran, on the other hand, is described as having gone to confession, a Catholic ritual, that involves telling a priest in the confession box what he has done—confessing his sin. The penance Doran's confessor would assign him (which is not indicated in the story) would normally be to say a number of prayers, which of course would not adequately balance out or repair the damage he has done—presumably getting Polly pregnant. We can't be sure about this, however; it might be simply that he had sex with her, and took her virginity, which, in Catholic Dublin in the early 1900s, would be enough for Mrs. Mooney to require a much more serious form of "reparation" than a few mumbled prayers: Doran's marrying her daughter.

Another aspect of setting is social register, with Doran occupying a higher rung in society than the Mooney family. Educated and in his thirties, he holds a good steady job, lives a regular life (having sowed his wild oats earlier), and is a desirable catch for a girl like Polly. Social status and society's influence figure as well in the close-knit world inhabited by the story's characters; people know one another's business. There's social pressure to do the right thing—not only from the determined Mrs. Mooney, but also from the snickering boarders and from Doran's boss, who exercises a different kind of influence on Doran, but one as powerful in its implications as those exerted by Mrs. Mooney and by Doran's own guilt-ridden conscience.

Point of View and Tone

Joyce's omniscient narrator enters the consciousness of each of the story's three main characters: Polly, Mrs. Mooney, and Bob Doran. The narrator reveals their thoughts and feelings to the reader. Imposing no limitations on his narrator, Joyce gives us insight into their state of mind, as, for example, with Mrs. Mooney, about whom he writes, "She was sure she would win." And about Mr. Doran, who "had a notion that he was being had." The narrator does the same with Polly, in effect, then, making us aware of multiple viewpoints, as he reveals the characters' differing perspectives on the situation. In the process, our sympathies shift from one character to another, as we come to understand their different needs and desires and hopes.

Joyce described the style of his *Dubliners* stories as one of "scrupulous meanness" (Ellmann 73). He meant by this that the stories presented a gritty reality of the lives of Dublin's people—across the social spectrum. He pulled no punches in showing the tawdry, dreary experiences of his Dubliners. And while the stories can't be considered "tragic," both individually and collectively they are certainly darkly sad in tone and temper.

Stylistically, Joyce employs a direct and forceful realism, something approaching naturalism, though without the tendency to exaggeration and distortion we find in naturalistic narratives like the novels of Theodore Dreiser and Honoré de Balzac. Joyce's sentences are direct and simple; they typically form a subject-verb-object pattern. His descriptions of character are straightforward, though with suggestive hints of judgment, as we noted earlier. The style suits the nature of the story's action; it is eminently compatible with the personalities of its characters; and it fits well with the restrictive circumstances of their lives.

There are brilliant touches in which Joyce shifts from description to dialogue. One notable example is the exchange Polly has with Mr. Doran, once they realize that they have gone too far (or just as far as they wished) sexually. Polly tells Doran that she has told her mother about their affair, and that Mrs. Mooney will speak with her lover in the morning. At this point Joyce describes her as throwing her arms around his neck, saying:

—O, Bob! Bob! What am I to do? What am I to do at all?
She would put an end to herself, she said.

The bit of direct speech is telling, its emphasis exclusively on Polly, though she should be saying something more like: "What are we to do?" "What can we do at all?" Joyce does not have her elaborate in her own words, shifting immediately, instead, to explanatory narrative, reporting rather than having her state that she will kill herself—a wild and hardly believable prospect given what we know of Polly.

With Doran's response, Joyce mixes narrative report ("He comforted her feebly") with a hint toward direct speech ("telling her not to cry," and "that it would be all right, never fear." In the same way that Joyce moves in and out of the consciousness (and conscience) of each of his characters, he moves into and out of their speech patterns, suggesting through description and omniscient report what they think and feel.

Thematic Implications

It would be a sin to reduce "The Boarding House" to an abstract thematic generalization, subsuming the richness of its situational complexity. It's a story, we might say, about how people's lives exist both in and out of their control, how their lives take turns for better and worse. It's a story, too, about the power and influence of religious and social ideology, and how those influences determine or at least forcefully influence people's decisions. They are shown making choices that affect their lives in ways they don't fully understand.

We may wonder, too, to what extent the story is about women's power over men, and about how women use their knowledge of men's weaknesses to get men to do their bidding. We may wonder to what extent this is a story about entrapment, about an unspoken yet conscious and intentional plan executed by Mrs. Mooney and Polly to achieve the end they both desire—Polly's marriage to a socially suitable partner.

An additional attraction of Joyce's *Dubliners* stories is how they work together to convey a rich picture of life in Dublin at the beginning of the twentieth century. Joyce weaves strands of style, imagery, symbol, and theme in complex ways, as each Dubliner story's characters and situations echo the others. Collectively, the stories provide glimpses of society high, middle, and low, as they portray characters in childhood, early adulthood, and middle and later age. Concrete details describing money and attire, drink and song, physical attributes and emotional states, assume symbolic weight across *Dubliners*. References to images of darkness and imprisonment, to religion and social status, are abundant, as "The Boarding House" amply demonstrates.

Reading Novel Openings

Wherever its opening pages take us—be it the fog-drenched streets of London in *Bleak House*, different forms of family disarray in *The Brothers Karamazov*, strange realms where clocks strike thirteen, or where hobbits live in their hobbit holes—a novel's beginning draws us into its unique world and establishes its special tone. It's worth taking time to absorb these novelistic elements, becoming familiar with what's distinctive about the work. In doing so we also become acquainted with a novel's major themes and preoccupations.

A slow, attentive reading of a novel's opening—whatever its length—prepares us for what's to come. Working carefully through a book's beginning alerts us to its language and tone, its milieu, while introducing its characters and establishing its subject(s) and prevailing conceptual center of gravity.

Here, for example, is the first chapter of Mark Twain's *Adventures of Huckleberry Finn*. In nine paragraphs Twain introduces the book's thematic preoccupations. In reading this opening chapter, we might keep the following questions in mind:

- What kind of narrative voice do we hear?
- What is the narrator's situation?
- What qualities of character does he possess?
- What subjects are raised and what attitudes are taken toward them?
- What might we predict will be some key thematic concerns of the novel?

You don't know about me without you have read a book by the name of "The Adventures of Tom Sawyer"; but that ain't no matter. That book was made by Mr. Mark Twain, and he told the truth, mainly. There was things which he stretched, but mainly he told the truth. That is nothing. I never seen anybody but lied one time or another, without it was Aunt Polly, or the widow, or maybe Mary. Aunt Polly—Tom's Aunt Polly, she is—and Mary, and the Widow Douglas is all told about in that book—which is mostly a true book; with some stretchers, as I said before.

Now the way that the book winds up, is this: Tom and me found the money that the robbers hid in the cave, and it made us rich. We got six thousand dollars apiece—all gold. It was an awful sight of money when it was piled up. Well, Judge Thatcher, he took it and put it out at interest, and it fetched us a dollar a day apiece, all the year round—more than a body could tell what to do with. The Widow Douglas, she took me for her son, and allowed she would sivilize me; but it was rough living in the house all the time, considering how dismal regular and decent the widow was in all her ways; and so when I couldn't stand it no longer, I lit out. I got into my old rags, and my sugar-hogshead again, and was free and satisfied. But Tom Sawyer, he hunted me up and said he was going to start a band of robbers, and I might join if I would go back to the widow and be respectable. So I went back.

The widow she cried over me, and called me a poor lost lamb, and she called me a lot of other names, too, but she never meant no harm by it. She put me in them new clothes again, and I couldn't do nothing but sweat and sweat, and feel all cramped up. Well, then, the old thing commenced again. The widow rung a bell for supper, and you had to come to time. When you got to the table you couldn't go right to eating, but you had to wait for the widow to tuck down her head and grumble a little over the victuals, though there warn't really anything the matter with them. That is, nothing only everything was cooked by itself. In a barrel of odds and ends it is different; things get mixed up, and the juice kind of swaps around, and the things go better.

After supper she got out her book and learned me about Moses and the Bulrushers, and I was in a sweat to find out all about him; but by and by she let it out that Moses had been dead a considerable long time; so then I didn't care no more about him; because I don't take no stock in dead people.

Pretty soon I wanted to smoke, and asked the widow to let me. But she wouldn't. She said it was a mean practice and wasn't clean, and I must try to not do it any more. That is just the way with some people. They get down on a thing when they don't know nothing about it. Here she was a-bothering about Moses, which was no kin to her, and no use to anybody, being gone, you see, yet finding a power of fault with me for doing a thing that had some good in it. And she took snuff, too; of course that was all right, because she done it herself.

Her sister, Miss Watson, a tolerable slim old maid, with goggles on, had just come to live with her, and took a set at me now with a spelling-book. She worked me middling hard for about an hour, and then the widow made her ease up. I couldn't stood it much longer. Then for an hour it was deadly dull, and I was fidgety. Miss Watson would say, "Don't put your feet up there, Huckleberry;" and "don't scrunch up like that, Huckleberry—set up straight;" and pretty soon she would say, "Don't gap and stretch like that, Huckleberry— why don't you try to behave?" Then she told me all about the bad place, and I said I wished I was there. She got mad then, but I didn't mean no harm. All I wanted was to go some- wheres; all I wanted was a change, I warn't particular. She said it was wicked to say what I said; said she wouldn't say it for the whole world; *she* was going to live so as to go to the good place. Well, I couldn't see no advantage in going where she was going, so I made up my mind I wouldn't try for it. But I never said so, because it would only make trouble, and wouldn't do no good.

Now she had got a start, and she went on and told me all about the good place. She said all a body would have to do there was to go around all day long with a harp and sing, for- ever and ever. So I didn't think much of it. But I never said so. I asked her if she reckoned Tom Sawyer would go there, and she said not by a considerable sight. I was glad about that, because I wanted him and me to be together.

Miss Watson she kept pecking at me, and it got tiresome and lonesome. By and by they fetched the niggers in and had prayers, and then everybody was off to bed. I went up to my room with a piece of candle and put it on the table. Then I set down in a chair by the window and tried to think of something cheerful, but it warn't no use. I felt so lonesome I most wished I was dead. The stars was shining, and the leaves rustled in the woods ever so mournful; and I heard an owl, away off, who-whooing about somebody that was dead, and a whippowill and a dog crying about somebody that was going to die; and the wind was trying to whisper something to me and I couldn't make out what it was, and so it made the cold shivers run over me. Then away out in the woods I heard that kind of a sound that a ghost makes when it wants to tell about something that's on its mind and can't make itself understood, and so can't rest easy in its grave, and has to go about that way every night grieving. I got so down-hearted and scared I did wish I had some company. Pretty soon a spider went crawling up my shoulder, and I flipped it off and it lit in the candle; and before I could budge it was all shriveled up. I didn't need anybody to tell me that that was an awful bad sign and would fetch me some bad luck, so I was scared and most shook the clothes off of me. I got up and turned around in my tracks three times and crossed my breast every time; and then I tied up a little lock of my hair with a thread to keep witches away. But I hadn't no confidence. You do that when you've lost a horseshoe that you've found, instead of nailing it up over the door, but I hadn't ever heard anybody say it was any way to keep off bad luck when you'd killed a spider.

I set down again, a-shaking all over, and got out my pipe for a smoke; for the house was all as still as death now, and so the widow wouldn't know. Well, after a long time I heard the clock away off in the town go boom—boom—boom—twelve licks—and all still again—stiller than ever. Pretty soon I heard a twig snap down in the dark amongst the trees—something was a stirring. I set still and listened. Directly I could just barely hear a *"me-yow! me-yow!"* down there. That was good! Says I, *"me-yow! me-yow!"* as soft as I could, and then I put out the light and scrambled out of the window on to the shed. Then I slipped down to the ground and crawled in among the trees, and, sure enough, there was Tom Sawyer waiting for me. (625–628)

COMMENTS

Through the first-person narrator, Huck Finn, Twain suggests that this will be a truthful book, one that describes honestly and accurately what the author knows. The implications of truth telling as a theme in the novel develop in different directions: truthfulness in the characters' relations with one another, truthfulness in honestly confronting oneself, and truthfulness in the way the novel reflects the world as Twain observes it. Huck mentions that everybody lies in one way or another at one time or another—with the possible exception of a few "good" people. In this way, Twain implies early on that though the novel will deal with the truth of things, it will depict various mendacious distortions of truth as well.

Another important feature of the opening paragraph is Twain's rendering of Huck's voice. We feel as if we are listening to someone talking to us. Huck's colloquial language, his grammatical lapses, his repetitions and interruptions contribute to the natural-sounding quality of his voice. So, too, does the regional dialect with which Twain imbues Huck's speech. When Ernest Hemingway remarked that all modern American literature derives from Twain's *Adventures of Huckleberry Finn*, one thing he had in mind, surely, was the realistic character of the book's many dialects and voices in a style William Giraldi describes as "fully embracing the linguistic grit and pitch of Americanese" (xxv).

With his references to Tom Sawyer, Twain introduces other key thematic preoccupations: the prominence of money and the conflict between the civilized and the natural world. Like Tom, Huck wishes to escape the constraints of domestic life. From his point of view, freedom outweighs the comforts of civilization. Huck's discomfort with the regular routines of home life anticipates his discomfort with other aspects of his experience, against which he will also rebel. Important thematically, too, is the way Huck's concern for freedom echoes what will become the novel's freedom-slavery opposition, which finds its dramatic center in the escaped slave Jim.

Yet another emphasis in the book's opening chapter is Huck's search for a father. The widow's taking Huck "for her son" suggests that Huck requires surrogate parenting. Judge Thatcher fulfills part of a father's responsibilities by watching over Huck's money. But we may wonder whether he or anyone else will provide the intellectual and moral guidance the young Huck needs. The search for a suitable father substitute becomes merged with the theme of freedom from slavery, as Twain establishes Jim as Huck's surrogate father.

Religion is a related concern, as well. From the widow's standpoint, Huck is a poor lost lamb, one who must return to the fold of obedient, civilized, churchgoing boys. She expects Huck not only to become accustomed to the social conventions of a regular dinner hour and proper attire, but also to participate in the ritual of offering a prayer of thanks before meals. As the novel develops, Twain will seriously challenge conventional religious attitudes and values. He will turn them inside out in a transvaluation through which decency, compassion, and true moral behavior are displayed courageously outside rather than within religious rituals and social conventions.

Especially important in this opening scene is the widow's threatening Huck with hell. Her threat backfires, as Huck, true to his sense of reality, prefers to go wherever she will not be—and where Tom Sawyer very likely will be—the "bad place." This scene anticipates what will later become a turning point in Huck's experience: the climactic scene in the novel when, confronted with the threat of hell via his socially conditioned conscience, Huck makes a decision that runs counter to everything he has been taught is morally right. The radical inversion of values that underlies so much of the book's trajectory of action appears in this opening chapter in attenuated, even comic form. Later it will be given more momentous treatment, in which Huck's decision of "uncut audacity" reflects his and the novel's assault on perverted values (Giraldi xxv).

And yet, as significant as these thematic strands may be, particularly as they adumbrate important ideas, it is less the ideas themselves than the ways they emerge through the particulars of plot and character, setting and point of view, voice and tone, that deserve our attention. Beyond thematic foreshadowing, Twain reveals Huck as a naive narrator who does not see what we readers see. This is the first of what will be numerous occasions in the novel in which a significant gap opens between what Huck understands and what readers understand. In that gap lies Twain's irony. Here in the opening chapter, the irony is relatively mild; later, it will become harsher and darker. This darker vision is hinted at even in this opening chapter with Huck's pragmatic independence and irreverence for Moses and other "dead people," for whom he has no use at all, whatever their historical or religious importance.

The book's initial chapter also reveals Huck's superstitious nature. For a boy who seems to question so much, to rebel against convention, and to challenge authority and received belief, Huck possesses a strong fear of what he does not understand. His superstitious nature suggests, perhaps, that he still has much to learn. Perhaps, too, it reveals an irreconcilable ambivalence in his way of looking at the world. On one hand, he seems clearheaded and skeptical; on the other, he is irrational. In either case, however, Huck's perceptions are sharp and vividly imagined.

In the expression of Huck's superstitious beliefs, as in his alertness to hypocrisy and his need for validation, Twain displays Huck's affinity for nature, an affinity that will find repeated expression as the novel develops. This affinity is powerfully evident in the splendid passages in which the river is shown to be a haven and refuge from the brutalities of an immoral, barbaric civilization, grounded in hypocrisy, cruelty, and greed.

Context and Intertext

In *World and Time: Teaching Literature in Context*, Adrian Barlow demonstrates the value of reading literary works in light of their own rich textures and in terms of other works to which they can be related. Barlow argues emphatically for the scrupulous close reading of a work, reading with care, respecting the author's intentions, and attending to nuances of language and form (29–35). In addition, he puts considerable weight on understanding a work's historical context, seeing it not so much from the perspective of our own time as from that of the time in which it was written (41–44, 86–102).

Barlow's attention to context and connection among literary works echoes the Anglo-American modernist T. S. Eliot's notion of the literary tradition. In his essay "Tradition and the Individual Talent," Eliot argued that every work of European literature exists in relation to every other work, and that works written today have an impact on the totality of literature, affecting the order of relations among works of the past, retroactively. Eliot describes the relationship among literary works as having a "simultaneous existence" and existing in a "simultaneous order" (4), though they were written centuries, even millennia apart. The more familiar understanding of literary tradition holds that works of the past influence those that come later, as Homer's *Iliad* and *Odyssey* influenced Virgil, and much later Joyce's *Ulysses*. Virgil's *Aeneid* influenced Dante, for another example, as Walt Whitman influenced future generations of twentieth-century American poets.

In *What Good Are the Arts?* John Carey puts a reader's personal, individual stamp on this process of literary influence when he notes that "our past reading becomes part of our imagination, and that is what we read with" (242). And again: "How we read . . . is affected by what we have read in the past" (242) along with how we have understood it and made that earlier reading meaningful for ourselves. In reading any literary work, we make connections with other works we have read, reading later ones in light of those we have read before, and understanding works read in the past in light of others read after them. In the process, we assemble what Carey describes as "our own literary canon" (242), a literary assemblage that is personally meaningful for each of us, individually.

In "The Community of Literature," Adrian Barlow proposes reading and teaching a cluster of novels in context, beginning with *Cutting for Stone* (2009) by Abraham Verghese, an American surgeon and a professor at the Stanford University Medical School.

Verghese was born in Ethiopia to parents from Kerala, India, who emigrated to the United States with their three children. Before completing his medical studies in India, Verghese worked in an American hospital as an orderly, an experience that he says made him a more compassionate physician and contributed to the slogan for his medical work: "Imagining the Patient's Experience" (Barlow, "The Community of Literature" 100).

These biographical details are relevant to *Cutting for Stone*, which moves, geographically, from India to Ethiopia, its primary setting, and to New York. Centered on hospitals in Ethiopia and America, both of which are understaffed and underresourced, the novel makes surgery a central motif and metaphor, dominating the life of its twin central characters. A further complication is the setting of the novel's African section amidst rebellion and civil war in Ethiopia.

Barlow recommends reading *Cutting for Stone* in terms of questions about colonialism and its consequences; immigration and its complications; cultural differences and complexity; radicalization; gender identity and gender politics; science and love, dramatized in the novel through issues of "twinship, kinship, and separation" (101). He proposes considering *Cutting for Stone* over against one or another of the following novels that describe similar issues of social taboos and cultural displacement.

Here are Barlow's suggestions for novel pairings:

- *The God of Small Things* (1997) by Arundhati Roy
  The legacy of empire and cruelties of the caste system. Twins experience severed parental and sibling relationships. Set in India.
- *White Teeth* (2005) by Zadie Smith
  West Indian, Bangladeshi, and English families over two generations. Twin sons—a radicalized Muslim and an atheist scientist. Set in London.
- *The Memory of Love* (2010) by Aminatta Forna
  The aftermath of civil war. A surgeon restores mutilated victims. A psychotherapist struggles to cope with the country's crisis. Set in Sierra Leone (101).

Putting stories and books into larger contexts, including seeing them in relation to one another, as Barlow emphatically notes, extends "the possibilities of dialogue between books and their readers and hence, fundamentally, to the idea of a community of literature" (102), one that enlarges and enriches the experience of every reader.

We can amplify the idea of literary community via Virginia Woolf's vision of readers across generations linked through their reading and interpretations of books. Woolf describes "minds threaded together across the centuries" and a "common mind that binds the whole world together" (cited in Bakewell 315). Sarah Bakewell suggests that it is the capacity for any particular book (she cites Montaigne's *Essais*) to live on in the minds of readers—to become a living part of their inner worlds—that joins those readers' minds in community.

And, finally, we should remember that a work of fiction, a single story, is never complete; it needs embellishment, elaboration, which we provide in imaginatively reenacting it. The book or story resonates with other books and stories and with other literary works within and beyond its genre. James Wood suggests that a story is never done, never over, never finished with itself or with us. Nor are we ever finished with a story; there's always more to say, to ask, to think, to wonder about (36). That's one additional pleasure that fiction affords us.

PART THREE Uses

FIVE   Reading's Paradoxical Pleasures

DIALECTICAL ENERGIES

Ideally, we lose ourselves in what we read, only to return to ourselves, transformed and part of a more expansive world.
—JUDITH BUTLER

Reading is often seen as a means to an end—to acquire information, amass knowledge, deepen understanding—all worthy goals, of course, for any reading, including the reading of literature. These goals, however, are frequently atomized, segregated, and made to serve limited purposes, including the development of reading "skills." Students, for example, are taught to "use" reading instead of to enjoy it; they are required to hunt for answers in texts, find the author's thesis, identify the main idea, locate the message, and the like. They are encouraged to put their reading to everyday use, including self-enhancement and self-improvement—again, certainly worthwhile reading goals. The practical approach to reading has its benefits for us all, to be sure, and I don't wish to deny its value. But I suggest that we can and do read for another valuable reason: to savor the experience of reading for itself, to succumb to reading's sundry seductive pleasures.

We read because we enjoy reading. We sometimes read from a sense of duty; more often we read out of a desire for pleasure: enjoyment motivates us more powerfully than does obligation.

But just what are the pleasures of reading? The primary pleasure of reading, including reading literature, is engaging with a text, immersing ourselves in it. We access its world and its thought. We savor its language and form. We absorb its vision and values. These aspects of reading extend beyond response and analysis.

We also connect productively with literary texts by relating them to our lives, linking them meaningfully with our experience of thinking and feeling and being. A troika of contemporary novelists provide different takes on what literary engagement does for readers. Jane Smiley suggests that reading literature is at once "an act of humanity . . . an act of connection . . . [and] an act of freedom" (253). Jeanette Winterson echoes Smiley by suggesting that books are "agents of freedom" (8). Through our reading we liberate ourselves; we access the minds of other human beings, minds that differ from ours, thus expanding our own minds in the process. Marilynne Robinson suggests, further, we experience literature's pleasures through enlarging the cultural mind and extending the capacities of language (321).

Beyond these manifestations of literary engagement is our involvement, through reading, with other people, including other writers, as we relate any particular text we read to other texts, other lives, other worlds of reading and of living experience. Reading literature widens our experience, giving us the opportunity to live other lives, visit other places, experience vicariously more than we ever could, directly, in our actual lives.

Discussing our reading with others, we discover that their experience of literary works will often differ from ours, partly corresponding to and partly diverging from our own. Conversations about our reading broaden and deepen our textual understanding, often prompting us to reread texts, to reconsider and reevaluate our initial take on them and our takeaways from them. Sometimes our rereading leads to shocks and recognitions that come from books we read long ago. Vivian Gornick describes her rereading of Natalia Ginzburg, whose work, Gornick notes, has always made her "love life more," in part through having her "eyes opened to something important about who [she] was at the moment of reading; later about who [she] was becoming" (101).

These forms of connection, moreover, are both emotional and intellectual; they engage the heart as well as the mind, our capacity for feeling as well as for thinking. The pleasures of feeling and of thinking exist reciprocally in mutual interplay; they stimulate, reinforce, and enrich one another. This is one of the most common and most significant of reading's complex pleasures. We value works of literature that compel us to think and to feel, that give us room to think even as we feel and to feel even while we think.

One of the best explanations for why and how literature, poetry especially, stimulates our minds and stirs our hearts comes from William Wordsworth's Preface to his *Lyrical Ballads*. In that revolutionary critical apologia, Wordsworth claims that "our continual influxes of feeling are modified and directed by our thoughts" (98). Wordsworth suggests that there is no such thing as pure unadulterated feeling, feeling unaffected by thought. And conversely, that there are no unadulterated thoughts—that our thoughts are embedded in and inflected by our past feelings. Feelings, over time, become thoughts; feeling recollected and contemplated becomes thought. Thought and feeling, thus, are cyclical and reciprocal, one inevitably following the other.

That's the first and one of the most important of reading's dialectical pleasures. A second is that to experience the pleasures of reading, especially of reading literature, we need, to a significant extent, to surrender ourselves to the text. We surrender, temporarily, to the writer's vision and the writer's values. We allow a book's language and form to do their work—to create a world of image and idea, of meaning and feeling and value(s), a world conjured with and through words. We submit ourselves to a work's ideas and values insofar as we understand them, after giving them our careful, patient, sustained attention—the purpose of that attention and effort to understand what the writer says and suggests, conveys and implies. Once we've done that, we can qualify, even resist, the text and its implications. One benefit of this dialectical response to our reading is that we learn from what we read even as we distance ourselves from it. We accept and appreciate it, and then critique and evaluate it. A double benefit, I think.

. . .

We engage in these acts of noticing, of making connections and inferences, slowly, deliberately, as if and in part to delay our full experience of the pleasures of textual understanding. That delay acknowledges the text's richness. Our attention to textual details, however, also prepares us for another of reading's pleasures—the pleasure of responding, of reacting to what we have so patiently and attentively submitted and surrendered to.

The pleasures of response are largely pleasures of assertion, of placing ourselves over against what we read. But this self-assertion, paradoxically, is most richly experienced, and most consummately rewarded, when coupled with the self-denial of textual surrender, with our submission to the text through careful, patient attention. This reciprocity between submission and resistance, acceptance and assertion, constitutes a second strand of reading's paradoxical pleasures.

Our involvement with a text, then (the root of our pleasure in reading), includes both an ability to restrain ourselves from responding to it, while permitting the text to work on us, and also an ability to assert ourselves over and against the text, testing it against our experience and knowledge, against other texts, as we compare it with their voices, visions, and values. The pleasures of delay, moreover, intensify the pleasures of response. In the process of delaying our response, we measure what the text sees and says and suggests, assessing its imaginings and assertions and values against our own, and against those of other texts we have read and absorbed. The temporary frustrations of reading lead, as Kenneth Burke suggests, to a more intense and complex set of satisfactions, a deeper and more pleasurable kind of fulfillment (*Counterstatement* 31). This, Burke argues, reflects a conception of form as the satisfaction of "desires and their appeasements" (31) and "the creation and satisfaction of needs" (138).

Response, of course, is postulated on recognizing an "other"—a voice, a figure, a character, a persona—as well as an actual author. There can be no pleasure of response without something to respond to, without someone to relate to. Paradoxically, in finding and recognizing this textual other, we find ourselves. The self we find, moreover, the self we perhaps (re)discover in the text, is enlarged through the process of engaging with and assimilating the text. We assimilate the work into ourselves, becoming absorbed in and through it—in yet another paradox of reading. We find ourselves in texts through losing ourselves in them—a third paradoxical and dialectical pleasure of reading.

Let's consider, briefly, the case of Montaigne's essays. A number of writers—Ralph Waldo Emerson, Virginia Woolf, and André

Gide among them—have suggested that in reading Montaigne's writing about himself, we become convinced we are reading about ourselves. Each individual reader encounters himself or herself while reading Montaigne's essays, even though those essays reveal Montaigne himself in all his splendid singularity. Montaigne's individuality, the minute particulars of mind he displays in essay after essay, was formed, paradoxically, through a study of ancient writers, primarily Roman, Latin having been his first language, serving his everyday needs as well as his educational ones, taking priority over French and the Gascon dialect of his native Bordeaux.

Montaigne said that he wrote about himself because he knew himself better than he knew anything or anyone else. In "Of Repentance," he writes: "[N]o man ever treated of a subject that he knew and understood better than I do this . . . and in this I am the most learned man alive" (611). Montaigne notes, however, that he exists in a state of flux: "I must adapt my history to the moment," he says, for "I may presently change, not only by chance, but also by intention" (611). "I do not portray being, but passing" (611), he writes. His essays, he claims, are "a record of diverse and changeable events, of undecided, and . . . contradictory ideas" (611). The title of his essay "On the Inconsistency of Our Actions" captures this sense of human variability. Who among us can deny seeing ourselves in Montaigne's characterization of his inconsistencies, his fluctuating feelings and attitudes, his momentary confusions and his repeated attempts to understand himself? And this in spite of his having been an aristocrat, a wealthy landowner, a civic administrator, and an able diplomat.

A reader's identity evolves through encountering, engaging with, and assimilating texts. We change along with the texts we read. Our reading of Montaigne's *Essais* at twenty or thirty is nothing like what we make of them two or three decades later. The reason simply is that when returning to literary works later in life we are neither the same readers nor the same people we once were. This change derives, in large part, from our deeper knowledge of life and of literature, of having read more, thought more, felt more, lived more. Neither we ourselves nor the literary works we read stand still or remain the same. We change and evolve together.

The pleasure of response, then, requires some kind of human connection, some recognition of the voice and value, some relation to the mind and heart of another, with some meaningful connection and, if we are lucky, even communion with the person on the other side of the reading transaction. The image of the individual reader absorbed in a book, addictively hooked, irretrievably lost, perhaps so fully transported that time seems to stop, remains a compelling one. In this image of reading, life seems deferred, the moment contracted, the reader entranced, enthralled, transported to another world, while the actual world of physical reality recedes, temporarily suspended. In "The House Was Quiet and the World Was Calm," Wallace Stevens describes such an engrossed reader, one who merges with the book being read. Unconscious of the book as a separate entity, Stevens's reader *becomes* the book; nothing separates them; there is no mediation; reader and book become *fused*, a single entity.

Even this seemingly most isolated of reading's pleasures, with the reader, solitary, immersed in the world of the book, does not do justice to reading's pleasures. This image of the individual reader reflects a partial perspective. An opposite perspective acknowledges that the sole reader, paradoxically, is not alone at all. Every true reader engaged in an authentic act of reading is connected, at least, minimally, with one other person—with the writer himself or herself (or the illusion of the writer, the trace of the writer), as well as with the speaker, narrator, and character(s) the work brings to life.

The reader's pleasures are not exclusively solitary pleasures; they are social pleasures as well—the pleasures of society beyond the reader's connection with the writer alone. These social pleasures manifest themselves in our conversations about and recommendations of books to friends and acquaintances. They are reflected in readers' joining together in book clubs run through schools and libraries and other civic associations. Will Schwalbe describes one such book club in his memoir, *The End of Your Life Book Club*, an unusual club with only two members, himself and his dying mother. Schwalbe reveals how he and his mother strengthened and deepened their relationship through their discussion of books.

Before the invention of print, reading was the quintessential social activity, as storytellers, lecturers, and priests read aloud to their varied congregations (Foer 226). That kind of early "reading"—listening really—was a passive collective experience. When the communal nature of reading (and being read to) gave way to private reading, reading became more intellectually active, with the resulting rifts opening a space for unorthodox thinking. Today we may engage more in forms of private, silent reading, especially when we read printed texts. But the social dimension of reading has not disappeared; it simply has taken other forms, including internet reading groups and other connecting structures technology has enabled.

Readers talk to one another, share their individual experience of reading this poem, that novel, this play, that essay. Readers seek confirmation of their own ways of understanding and experiencing a particular work. When they find it, they feel vindicated, the reinforcement of others' experience supporting and validating their own. When they don't find it, interesting discussions ensue. Why didn't you see this work the way I did? What did you notice that I missed? What did we both see that we understand in such different ways? From questions like these, readers extend their ways of seeing and thinking, and they increase their initial reading pleasure.

The concentrating, concentrated reader becomes the connected, communing reader. The isolation of a single reader morphs into communication among multiple readers. Reading as a solitary, self-intensive pleasure and reading as a social, self-transcending experience together capture, then, yet another kind of reading duality, the fourth of reading's paradoxical, dialectical pleasures. In the next part of this chapter, I identify nine (and a half) additional related dialectical and pleasurable tensions we experience in the act of reading.

. . .

Before doing that, however, I need to establish a number of assumptions about reading literature. First, I assume that whatever their genre, literary works *mean* something and that those meanings are recoverable, multiple, and many-faceted, and not elusive, singular, and one-dimensional.

Second, I assume that the meaning of a work includes more than its animating intellectual idea or its generalizable content. A work's meaning also includes our experience of reading it, both the experience of reading during our actual encounter with the work in real time and our residual experience of it in memory.

Third, recapitulating something explored earlier, I suggest that a work's meaning includes our emotional apprehension as well as our intellectual comprehension of it. Our understanding of literary works encompasses our full human response, emotive as well as cognitive. Thought embodied in feeling; feeling refracted through thought.

And, fourth, I assume that the meaning of literary works includes what they *do* to us as well as what they *say* to us. Their meanings, thus, include significant real-life consequences; they affect not only our ideas but also our decisions and our actions. We define ourselves in relation to certain books. As Italo Calvino reminds us, certain books—literary classics especially—"help us understand who we are and where we stand" (133); they contribute to making us who we are and who we will become.

Now these assumptions might seem to suggest that the meaning of a story, for example, lies in the reader, since it is the reader who experiences the responses of thought and feeling the work evokes. Some reader-response and reception theorists, including Wolfgang Iser, suggest that literary meaning resides neither in the reader nor in the text but in the "interaction" (Iser's word) that exists between text and reader. Unlike theorists who assume that the text can mean anything the reader makes it mean (relativists), or those who assume it means essentially nothing because it constantly undermines itself (deconstructionists), Iser recognizes the importance of the text in guiding, checking, and otherwise constraining the reader's interpretive efforts.

Iser invokes the common notion that "[t]he [literary] work is more than the text, for the text only takes on life when it is realized" (*Implied Reader* 274). I have trouble with Iser on this point, as he distinguishes text from work, arguing that literary works do not exist until they are brought to life by readers. I certainly agree that there is more to a literary work than the words on a page. I agree, too, that readers bring literary works to life. But those works also exist in their own right by virtue of their authors having created them. The first to experience the works and endow them with life are the very authors that Iser's theoretical distinction between text and work would diminish, if not abolish. Authors deserve double credit—first for creating their works and next for being their first readers. Iser seems to deny to literary works an independent existence, thereby devaluing their author's achievement, while simultaneously exalting readers through making them cocreators with the authors whose works they read. This perspective, I think, gives readers too much credit and authors too little.

In performing literary works, readers remake them and bring them to renewed life. Rather than creating literary works ex nihilo, readers re-create what authors have made. And under the best of conditions they re-create themselves in the process.

As Iser suggests, an author provides a coherent pattern and a suitable context for the reader's imaginative completion of the work's suggestive implications. The text comes to life only "when it is realized," a textual "realization" that reflects the "esthetic" pole of the literary work, and the author's actual created work, the "artistic" pole (*The Act of Reading* 21).

Iser also describes how readers build consistency as they read, looking for ways to unify textual variety into a coherent whole. He suggests that a successful reading finds a balance between the opposed factors of the polysemantic nature of literary works and the illusion-making faculty of readers (*Implied Reader* 284), with the potential text infinitely richer than any of its individual realizations. The text proposes, the reader disposes—but only within the boundaries the text encloses. The reader constructs as the text instructs—though carefully acknowledging the text's restrictions.

. . .

Where does this leave us, as readers, in our relation to texts? It leaves us where we often find ourselves after an excursion, however brief, into theory—with a need to formulate a clear and direct approach to literary interpretation. It leaves us with the need to balance the competing pressures theorists like Iser describe. We need to decide when to assert ourselves against a text and when to submit to it—and how to do both. We need, as well, to listen to the text before speaking back to or against it. We can follow the lead of the text, deciding where and when to diverge from it—and why—as I have been trying to do myself, here, in my dialogue with Iser. We can do these things by identifying and balancing the various tensions we experience in reading. These tensions constitute additional paradoxically dialectical reading pleasures, additions to the four previously described.

- First, the tension between "text" and "work," the black marks on the white page ("text"), and the version of the work we readers bring to life in our minds as we read ("work"). Or, alternatively, the tension between the work as *created* by the author and the work as *re-created* by the reader.

- Second, the tension between the temporal flow of reading—making sense *as we go* through the text—and making additional sense *in retrospect*, in the tranquility of postreading reflection. Forward and backward reading. The tension between the text in motion and the text at rest.

- Third, the tension between the pleasures associated with *finality* and those associated with *deferral*; the delights of progressing slowly and forestalling, and thereby heightening, the pleasures of closure. And the pleasure of ending, finishing, concluding.

- Fourth, the tension between the text as a *mirror* in which we see ourselves and the text as a *window* into a strange other world, which is both disorienting and exciting as we encounter that world and the "other" in it. The tension between reading toward the *self* and reading toward the *world*.

- Between fourth and fifth—four and a half—the tension between the text as *visible* and *invisible*—as an *artifact* you examine and as a *place in which you lose yourself* in its story and its world. "Foregrounding the text as an object of interest," as Lydia Davis notes (223); and losing sight of your discriminating mind while reading.

- Fifth, the tension between *author consciousness* and *reader consciousness*, between *mindlessness*—giving your mind over to the author—and *mindfulness*—maintaining control of your mind; a tension related to that of submission and resistance.

- Sixth, the tension between the formation and the breaking of illusions; the tension between *suspending* and *asserting disbelief*. The tension between skepticism and belief, between doubt and trust.

- Seventh, the tension between the *implied reader* and the *actual reader*; the gap between what the text requires of us and what we bring to texts and make of them in all our idiosyncratic particularity. The tension between the potential and the actual, the ideal reader and actual readers.

- Eighth, the tension between the text/work as *finished* and the text/work as *unfinished*—the *closed* versus the *open* work.

- And ninth, the tension between the work as an *independent self-contained* aesthetic object and the work as *embedded, contextualized* in a larger social structure. The text as a singular self-enclosed authorial production and the text as a relational social artifact with ties to the world.

These oppositional strains pull *inward* toward the reader's concerns, and they push *outward*, away from the self-centered reader, taking readers beyond themselves. Reading exists on a continuum of textual practices—from experience to analysis, subjectivity to objectivity, impression to interpretation to critical evaluation. On one hand, reading looks into textual relationships within a work—images, details, actions, and other patterns—*intra*textual reading. On the other hand, reading looks toward textual connections outside a work, between and among the individual work and other works and contexts—*inter*textual reading. It's not that one kind of reading is good and the other bad, one to be avoided, the other embraced. Both approaches are useful in their place and for their particular purposes. Inward-directed and outward-directed reading complement and reinforce each other. They deepen each other, enrich each other, complete each other. Theirs is a dialectical relationship, a marriage of reconcilable dualities, a harmonious yin-yang balance.

To ignore these oppositions, to explain away the tensions they embody, impoverishes our understanding of literature and limits our ability to realize and fully enjoy its many paradoxical pleasures. The tensions between textual responsiveness and responsibility—between the entitlements of the author and those of the reader—need to be acknowledged and negotiated. Their competing claims need to be satisfactorily adjudicated, as they underlie any convincing theory and any productive practice of reading.

Henry James has written that in reading a work of literature, a novel in particular, we live "another life for a short while," an experience that results in an enlargement of our world and our life (93). I believe that James is right, and that by balancing the various tensions in reading literary works that I have described, we can live multiple other lives, broadening and deepening our virtual and vicarious experience through the dialectical, paradoxical pleasures reading literature so gloriously affords us.

six Reading for Your Life

HOW READING IS ENTWINED WITH LIVING

And no doubt that is what reading is: rewriting the text of the work within the text of our lives.
—ROLAND BARTHES

What Good Is Literature?

Literature serves three broad purposes: to instruct, to delight, and to move; literature teaches, entertains, and engages us intellectually and emotionally. We might call these three effects the uses of literature. In this chapter, I consider some additional uses literature has for readers, and I explore some ways literature links up with our lives.

Beyond instruction, pleasure, and engagement, what else can literature offer us? It offers us the chance to develop discernment and literary tact—the opportunity to enhance our critical capacities. This can take a lifetime to master.

Additionally, we might ask how literature affects us, and why that matters. One answer is that literature helps us live our lives. A related answer is that literature offers us a vision of life—various visions of life's possibilities. But what do these answers mean, specifically, and in practice?

In *Books for Living*, Will Schwalbe claims that reading is among the best ways we have to examine our lives. Through comparing ourselves with literary characters—with what they do and don't do, with what motivates them to behave as they do, with how they feel and think—we learn about ourselves. Reading also, he suggests, reduces loneliness in connecting us with others. And, in a time of frenzied 24/7 activity, Schwalbe argues for reading books as a way to "change our relationship to the rhythms and habits of daily life" (14). Books demand our attention; they require that we stop what we're doing, that we focus on them. Books make us listen to what their authors have to say—even when an author's book angers us,

149

infuriates us, goes against the grain of our thinking or beliefs. As I suggested in chapter 2, "Reading for the Truth," books help us become who we are. They become inextricably entwined with our lives. We can't escape their influence, nor would we want to. We become what we read.

In telling their stories, books tell us stories about ourselves. We can read toward self-knowledge and learn things about ourselves previously unrecognized. Support for this notion comes from none other than Marcel Proust. In *Poetics of Reading*, Inge Wimmers quotes a passage from Proust's *In Search of Lost Time*. Here is her translation: "In reality, every reader is, while he is reading, the reader of his own self. The writer's work is merely a kind of optical instrument which he offers to the reader to enable him to discern what, without this book, he would perhaps never have perceived in himself" (10–11). Books, as Proust claims, let us see ourselves in ways unavailable without their agency.

In *Reading through the Night*, Jane Tompkins echoes the thinking of Proust's narrator, as she emphasizes how reading affects not only our self-knowledge but also our feelings about ourselves. She explores reading's therapeutic effects. A long and debilitating illness prodded Tompkins into a way of reading that changed her relationship to the books she read and to herself as a reader. Where she had once read as a way to find refuge or adventure, and as a literary and cultural critic, Tompkins began reading later in life for self-understanding. Revelations came to her unexpectedly from bits of dialogue or description, evoking feelings and thoughts previously unnoticed or repressed. Tompkins expanded the roles books played in her life to include reading's effects on her energy level, and as a spur to change her thinking and behavior. A book became for her a path to transformation and "an instrument of realization" (16).

Reading this way serves as a stimulus to self-reflection. Reading becomes a form of therapy—bibliotherapy. We can accept or reject what books tell us; we can change ourselves in response to them or not. But their therapeutic potential exists, nonetheless.

And yet if we read to be taken *into* ourselves, we also read to be taken *out* of ourselves, a paradox of reading related to those described in the previous chapter. In *American Audacity*, William

Giraldi reminds us that "[l]iterature both leads us forth from our-selves and returns us to ourselves" (xxix). He suggests further that great books are not "echo chambers where we hear ourselves am-plified"; instead, they "allow us to partake of what we are not and can never be" (xxix). Contemporary novelist Richard Russo sug-gests that getting lost in a literary work, a good story especially, is "an antidote to self-consciousness." And perhaps to solipsism as well.

Recognizing ourselves in books involves moments of personal illumination that lead to deepened self-understanding. Reading provides opportunities not only to increase our knowledge but to improve our judgment. It provides occasions for discernment. Reading literature also demonstrates how recognizing others can lead to acceptance and toleration. Because the fresh ways of seeing that literature offers are embedded in affiliations we have with others across the spectrum of our social lives, recognizing our-selves in literary works represents more than personal epiphanies. Literary works implicate us simultaneously in "circles of acknowl-edgment" that draw from and stretch across a broad swath of social life (Felski 48).

Rita Felski asks readers to consider why they are drawn to liter-ary works in the first place. She asks this question not only of gen-eral readers, but of professional readers as well, including literary critics, who espouse particular literary theoretical approaches to analyzing and interpreting texts. Positioning herself against those who endorse poses of "analytical detachment, critical vigilance, guarded suspicion" (2), Felski asks her readers to consider what practical value they gain from reading literature. One such value, surely, is that from reading literature we learn how to live. We learn about ourselves and about our human potential; we learn, too, about our limitations and deficiencies. Literary works are forma-tive, serving as sources as well as objects of knowledge (7). We can learn from them because they foster fresh ways of seeing, irrespec-tive of political, social, theological, or other ideological uses to which literary texts can be and often are put. "We make ourselves," she contends, "out of the models we encounter; we give ourselves a form through the different ways we inhabit other forms" (172). Our encounters with works of literature shape and reshape us, orient and reorient us (172). They contribute immeasurably to the selves we become. And this is so because, paradoxically, as we absorb them and assimilate them, we go beyond them, using them for our distinctive purposes.

Among the most distinctive of such purposes are those Ralph James Savarese describes in *See It Feelingly*, a book about his experience reading literature with autistic adults. Savarese worked with each of his readers individually in tutorial fashion, sometimes in person, sometimes typing online, and sometimes via Skype. They read and discussed together a chapter or two per week of classic and contemporary American works that included *Moby-Dick*, *Adventures of Huckleberry Finn*, *The Heart Is a Lonely Hunter*, *Ceremony*, and *Do Androids Dream of Electric Sheep?*, inspiration for the Ridley Scott film *Blade Runner*.

Discussing the works over a period of years with readers across the autistic spectrum, Savarese was amazed at their ability to expand his understanding of books he had taught for decades. Savarese argues that his readers' perceptions derive not only from the different ways their minds and bodies respond to literature, but also from their experiences of stigma and exclusion. His autistic students revealed themselves to be the most empathetic and engaged of readers, connecting with literary works in ways that both surprised and amazed him.

Savarese's discoveries about the autistic imagination and the rich variety of ways his students relate to works of literature have something to teach us about what creative and imaginative reading and teaching can be. His ethnographic research with his highly individual readers and their acute insights provide evidence that the ways readers experience, understand, and use literary works are far more various, interesting, and inspiring than we might imagine. *See It Feelingly* (the book's title derives from *King Lear*) demonstrates in just one of many possible ways that literature changes how we see the world, altering our perception of life in general and of our own lives in particular—how each person's life circumstances influence his or her reading of literature.

John Carey emphasizes yet another value of reading literature. In *What Good Are the Arts?*, Carey stresses literature's power to stimulate critical thinking. Carey values literature for its powers of reasoning: "the only art capable of reasoning" (177), he avers. For Carey, literature is superior to other writing, and to all the arts, because it makes readers reflect; it develops their imaginations and encourages self-critical thought. Literature stocks our minds with ideas. Literature helps us think broadly and deeply because it is rife with complexity and counterargument, "reappraisal and qualification" (208). An effective tool for thinking, literature questions and challenges as it describes and portrays. As a force for developing the mind, literature, Carey suggests, "strengthens our sense of selfhood and individuality" while enhancing our "private, individual imagining" (213). As Robert Eaglestone notes, through reading literature "we make ourselves intelligible to ourselves" (1), yet another affiliated way of characterizing literature's power to enforce self-understanding.

Literature remains open to interpretative possibilities, to unpredictable readings, to a range of uses to which it can be put, including moral uses, as exemplified by many writers, Jane Austen and Michel de Montaigne, famously, among them. While Austen and Montaigne don't instruct readers directly and counsel them to behave one way or another, they do so indirectly, by exemplifying how to live productively and happily in society, Montaigne through historical reference, Austen through her characters' actions. As if glossing Montaigne and Austen, Terry Eagleton suggests that "literature improves us morally by making us more self-critical, self-conscious, flexible, provisional, open-minded and robustly skeptical of orthodoxies" (104). These large claims, of course, can be proven only in the practice of reading literature; they can be endorsed or challenged by each reader in the cauldron of his or her literary experience.

Literature as a Never-Ending Conversation

Literature has long been the source of an ongoing conversation to which all readers are invited. This type of informed conversation about books and ideas lies at the heart of a liberal education. In *The Philosophy of Literary Form*, Kenneth Burke describes the exchange of ideas as a never-ending conversation. Here is the scene Burke conjures as he asks his readers to imagine entering a room:

> You come late. When you arrive, others have long preceded you, and they are engaged in a heated discussion. . . . You listen for a while, until you decide that you have caught the tenor of the argument; then you put in your oar. Someone answers; you answer him; another comes to your defense; another aligns himself against you. . . . The hour grows late, you must depart. And you do depart, with the discussion still vigorously in progress. (*Philosophy* 110–111)

Literature provides a source of continuing opportunities to participate in this kind of mind-stretching conversation, a dialogue among books and authors that has been going on for millennia. We might ask ourselves what our relationship with books—especially with literature and, more particularly, with good and great literature—might be.

Among the earliest models of education as conversation is that of Petrarch, who revered the ancients and wanted to restore the glory of the Greco-Roman past. Enamored of the Latin writers, Cicero, especially, Petrarch wrote them letters. And though they couldn't write back, he could imagine their responses based on what he read in their works. Another example can be found in the reading habits of Niccolò Machiavelli, who would don his best clothes before sitting down to read the classical writers of ancient Greece and Rome. While reading ancient literature and philosophy, Machiavelli imagined himself in conversation with writers such as Caesar and Cicero, Homer and Horace, Seneca and Sophocles. Readers of Machiavelli's political work *The Prince* or his play *La Mandragola* engage in conversation with him as he did with the ancient writers.

A few centuries after Machiavelli, Henry David Thoreau, in his most celebrated work, *Walden*, describes how he began each morning with a reading of ancient works and a walk to Walden Pond. He imagined himself in communion with earlier civilizations as he bathed in the pond, linking himself with those who purified themselves spiritually in the River Ganges in India. Thoreau imagined the ancient Greek warriors of Homer's *Iliad* as he watched and described a ferocious battle between red and black ants, comparing the torn and defeated insect combatants to the Greek and Trojan warriors of antiquity.

Petrarch, Machiavelli, and Thoreau illustrate how reading can be both a solitary pursuit and a social one. Petrarch inaugurated the systematic study of the ancient writers that launched the Italian Renaissance. Machiavelli served as an adviser to the Medici, and Thoreau shared his knowledge and love of the classics through public lectures. Their books extended their influence. Petrarch's *Canzoniere* inaugurated a poetic movement emphasizing the love of a distant and unattainable ideal woman. Machiavelli's *The Prince* has long remained a guide to how to acquire and maintain political power. Thoreau's *Walden* remains a guide to living, one that strongly influenced Leo Tolstoy, Mahatma Gandhi, and Martin Luther King, Jr.

One way of thinking about the process of reading itself is as a kind of conversation. It's an encounter between two persons—writer and reader, one writer, one reader at a time. We gain from these conversations both companionship and solace.

But how do we engage with authors and their works? One way is to make notes in the margins of books we own. We can respond to the ideas of authors, engage with their thinking, talk back to them, extend their thinking by borrowing their ideas and applying them to new situations. And we can continue our private discussions in conversation with others, which almost always enrich our own literary experience.

Our dialogue with literary works continues all our lives; the books we read speak to each other as well as to us. Great books adapt to us; as Ali Smith notes, "[T]hey alter with us as we alter in life, they renew themselves as we change and re-read them at different times of our lives" (32–33). And just as you can't step into the same river twice, you also "can't step into the same story twice," nor can great books and stories "step into the same person twice" (33). We can't step into the same book twice because the book we have read and then read again changes for us as we change. Although the words are the same, they mean something different for us at different stages of our lives.

We learn to read books we encountered when young with our later more developed selves. The books don't stand still any more than we do. And the greatest of those books read us in return. We are read by the books we read; the great writers—novelists, poets, dramatists, essayists—know us better than we know ourselves. And that is the case, paradoxically, even as the texts of the literary works remain the same—what they have always been, and always will be, regardless of what readers continue to make of them. The text remains, but the work changes. The words remain, but their meaning is transformed.

Literature accomplishes these things by inciting our imaginative participation in the lives of others. We project ourselves into other worlds, other lives, other ways of thinking and feeling—and thereby extend the range of our own experience. In his novel *Brooklyn*, for one of many examples we might choose, Colm Tóibín tells the story of a young Irish immigrant woman, Eilis Lacey, who leaves her homeland, travels by ship, and arrives in Brooklyn, New York, after World War II, to make a life for herself. Through reading Tóibín's imaginative re-creation of Eilis's experience, we come to understand intellectually and emotionally what it was like for her—what she thought and felt back in Ireland, then during her sea journey, and, finally, later in America. We see through her eyes; we share her shifting emotions; we understand and live through her experience imaginatively—regardless of our age, gender, race, or ethnicity.

Reading well deepens understanding and extends thinking. Reading stirs us into thought both critical and creative; it incites reflection and wonder, admiration and critical response. It sets us on trails of thought we didn't know we were going to follow, communicating things even its author may not realize have been suggested, saying something its author perhaps neither intended nor set out to say (Calvino 99). Reading also brings to mind fragments of our previously forgotten experience, "intuitions and half-recognitions that may still remain shadowy, inexplicit, or under-appreciated" (Philip Davis 73). Literature frequently surprises us; sometimes this surprise results in our becoming aware, or quasi-aware, of something we didn't know we knew, of something we had forgotten how to feel, something retrieved from memory, however haltingly.

Our acts of reading, like the literary works we read, are performances, which are self-delighting. To achieve this level of literary pleasure, our reading of literature requires that we engage it on its own terms, that we take it playfully yet seriously, that we bring to bear the full range of our knowledge and experience so as to take from it all it has to offer, to make of it as much as we possibly can for our own sake, for the sake of the work itself, and the worlds of literature, language, and life to which it belongs.

Reading and the Quality of Life

How many lives have been altered by the reading of a book? How many ideas and experiences have been startled into life by something someone read? How much has reading stimulated us by provoking us to think, motivating us to act, inspiring us to change our ways of thinking and acting? Reading alters lives.

Those who experience the pleasures and powers of reading early carry them into their later lives, as athletes carry to adulthood skills developed playing sports in their youth. Reading, like certain sports—tennis, swimming, skiing, and golf, among them—can be learned early and continued throughout one's lifetime. An ability to read perceptively identifies a person as educated, and likely interesting. An ability to read with understanding and enjoyment provides a source of lifelong pleasure.

And yet all the arguments we might make for reading well—the pragmatic argument about its usefulness in school and at work, and the experiential arguments about how reading brings manifold pleasures throughout our lives—are not enough to account for its value and its importance. Reading is worthwhile, paradoxically, because it is not absolutely essential for living—it's not like breathing; it's not required for getting on in life. Many people succeed without doing much reading. Reading well will not guarantee fame or fortune, nor can it ensure worldly success.

Reading is a luxury more than a necessity, though one, certainly, that enriches our lives. Reading makes us more interesting to ourselves, better company for ourselves—and better company for others as well. Reading helps us to have more beautiful minds.

Reading can inspire us in a multitude of ways. In Iceland reading inspires not only more reading, but also lots of writing. With a 100 percent literacy rate among its citizens, every Icelander can enjoy the great sagas of early Icelandic myth and history. The populace has been inspired by those magisterial works, as well as by an 1854 Icelandic language Bible that was a required purchase for every parish church in the country, and which is now housed in the Skógar Museum. Icelanders are not only great readers, but also frequent writers. Fully 10 percent of Icelanders today are expected not only to write a book but to publish one in their lifetimes. The country considers itself a *bokathjod*, or book nation. According to a recent *Wall Street Journal Review* article, books have been key to the country's survival, insofar as no matter the extent of people's pain or poverty, they consistently have found solace in books (A. Kendra Greene C3).

In *A Moveable Feast*, Ernest Hemingway describes his early adulthood as a developing writer living as an expat in Paris. What made the poverty of his early Paris years tolerable, even pleasurable, were books—books Hemingway was lent by the gracious Sylvia Beach at her landmark Parisian bookstore, Shakespeare & Company. Hemingway borrowed many books from that store; he describes with joy the writers and their worlds he discovered there—among them the great nineteenth-century French and Russian novelists and short story writers then being translated into English: Balzac, Flaubert, and de Maupassant; Tolstoy, Dostoyevsky, and Chekhov, especially. These writers helped Hemingway become the writer he did, less through imitation than inspiration.

Ars longa, vita brevis—art is long, life is short, writes Seneca in *On the Shortness of Life*. And yet we might also argue that life is long and getting longer. Once formal schooling is finished, many years of living and working typically lie ahead of us. What are we to do with our leisure during those years? How are we to spend our time beyond the hours we invest in working, however fulfilling our jobs and careers might be? Mass entertainment, of course, beckons: movies, television, spectator sports; the internet, smartphones, and other technological marvels, to say nothing of traveling and socializing, playing games and sports, engaging in hobbies.

Without casting aspersions on any of these pleasurable activities, we also have reading, the kind of reading that keeps our minds actively learning about all manner of things, practical and impractical, some directly of use to us, others of no earthly use at all. It is the reading we do for ourselves because we want to, rather than because we need to, that helps us not only to pass the time, but also to sharpen and deepen our perception of the world and better understand our place in it. Literature best satisfies these disparate needs.

Living with Literature

Literature itself is a form of experience, an experience of living through language. Moreover, literature is not a virtual experience, but rather an actual experience of our lives, a form and aspect of life itself.

Kenneth Burke has described literature as "equipment for living" (*Philosophy* 253), and Jeanette Winterson as both a "compass" and a "tool kit" (8). Depending on what we consider to be the uses of literature for our everyday lives, and what we understand fundamentally by the concept of utility, we may agree more or less with one or another of these definitions of literature. There is no question, though, that literature can provide us with ways to enlarge and deepen our understanding, and, in so doing, provide us with strategies for living our lives more fully and rewardingly.

We consider, next, a range of ways literature can prove valuable for living. Our brief excursion takes us through recent books about how an author or book changed a writer's life and can change others' lives. Titles include *How Proust Can Change Your Life*, *How to Live*, *An Odyssey*, *My Life in Middlemarch*, *Give War and Peace a Chance*, *Reading Dante*, and *In a Dark Wood*, a book also inspired by Dante.

Although the authors of these books differ in approach, each explores how a writer's masterpiece remains relevant for people's lives today. They are interested, respectively, in how Proust, Montaigne, Homer, Eliot, Tolstoy, and Dante engage readers in the twenty-first century.

In *How Proust Can Change Your Life*, Alain de Botton shows how Proust understood the importance of small routines and daily rituals. De Botton uses Proust's seven-volume novel, *In Search of Lost Time* (also translated as *Remembrance of Things Past*), as a guide to living, including how to revive a relationship, enjoy a vacation, recognize love, and be a good host. Proust's many bodily ailments, including his chronic asthma, serve as fodder for de Botton on how to deal with physical pain and with bad neighbors as well. De Botton explicates Proust's themes—time, love, friendship, literature—revealing less about Proust's novel than about the author's life. While parodying self-help books, de Botton writes one; while playfully recontextualizing a literary monument more often talked about than read, he incites us to read Proust and to consider how literature provides both pleasure and help in our everyday lives.

In her book on Montaigne's life and writing, *How to Live*, Sarah Bakewell finds an even greater range of helpful advice. Addressing the question of how to live, she explores twenty answers, playing on the meaning of "essay" as a "try," an "attempt," and a "taste." Bakewell offers twenty "attempts at an answer" based on Montaigne's 107 essays. Among them are these: be born; pay attention; use little tricks; don't worry about death; question everything; be convivial; live temperately; see the world; do something no one has done before; do a good job, but not too good a job; give up control; reflect on everything, regret nothing; be ordinary and imperfect; let life be its own answer. Lots of good advice, surely, if only we might follow it. We read Montaigne as he wrestles with these questions in his own life; we read him for his serenity, his sanity, his honesty, his humanity—to say nothing of his artistry and his rhetorical mastery. We read him for his essaying of himself, of what it means to be human in a complex and ever-changing world—both his world and ours.

Why read Montaigne? We read Montaigne, as Flaubert has written, "in order to live" (cited in Bakewell 9). For Montaigne, it is not what he does that matters, but who he is. His essays express not only his thinking and his feelings, but his very being. Montaigne is consubstantial with his book. In reading it we find him; paradoxically, we also find ourselves.

If Montaigne is synonymous with essay, Homer holds that honor for epic, his *Iliad* and *Odyssey* influencing every epic in the Western world afterward. Daniel Mendelsohn's *An Odyssey* celebrates Homer's popular work through recounting his course on the epic at Bard College, offering an interpretation of the work, and penning a memoir about his father, including their shared experience of reading the *Odyssey*, and of an Ionian cruise they took that followed in the wake of Odysseus. Melding memoir with literary criticism and pedagogical instruction, Mendelsohn elucidates the major concerns of the *Odyssey*: deception and recognition; courage and cowardice; the relationships between fathers and sons, and between husbands and wives; the inducements of travel; and the meaning of home. Along the way, Mendelsohn reflects on his own life, especially his complex relationship with his father and his more comfortable relationship with his students, both of which he dramatizes in his book.

Perhaps the genre most frequently cited by authors who relate their lives with literature is the novel. Among the works featured in recent books whose authors have made the novel a significant facet of their personal and thinking lives are George Eliot's *Middlemarch*, which Virginia Woolf described as "one of the few English novels written for grown-up people" ("George Eliot" 175), and Tolstoy's *War and Peace*, which many regard as the greatest novel ever written in any language.

In *My Life in Middlemarch*, Rebecca Mead describes her love affair with Eliot's book, which began when she was an undergraduate and continued throughout her early and later adult life. Mead blends biography, literary criticism, journalism, and memoir in exploring the themes of *Middlemarch* and of her own life—the complications of love, the meaning and value of marriage, the bases of morality, the challenges of ambition and failure. Through her investigation of these themes in Eliot's novel and in her own life and marriage, Mead brings *Middlemarch* into our time and place. While doing so, she brings the magisterial work down to earth and close to home, showing how in reading a great book well, we also enable it to read ourselves.

A Random House survey of one hundred of the world's greatest and most important novels placed *War and Peace* first. The size, scope, and scale of *War and Peace* have not frightened readers away, nor have they intimidated translators. What keeps readers coming to this mega-novel? Some reasons are suggested by Andrew D. Kaufman in *Give War and Peace a Chance*. Kaufman notes that *War and Peace* is many things, including, of course, a war novel. But it is also a family saga, a love story, and a book about people "attempting to create a meaningful life for themselves in a country being torn apart by war, social change, and spiritual confusion" (5). Our situation, to some extent at least, mirrors the world of early nineteenth-century Russia that Tolstoy describes. His characters are much like us in the kinds of mistakes they make, the ways they suffer—at their own hands as well as those of others—and how they cope with their errors and their pain. When they are lucky, they experience moments of transcendence. At these times Tolstoy's characters' lives are momentarily suspended, as they become more acutely awakened to life's beauties; their perceptions are sharpened, their feelings deepened, their sense of life expanded and heightened.

In capturing the richness and depth of *War and Peace*, Kaufman organizes his book according to the novel's major thematic preoccupations. His chapter titles identify these themes: plans, imagination, rupture, success, idealism, happiness, love, family, courage, death, perseverance, and truth. In exploring these broad themes, Kaufman's mixed-genre book, which includes biography, history, philosophy, and literary appreciation, invites us to accompany Tolstoy on his search for answers to life's big questions: Who am I? Why am I here? How should I live?

What could be more relevant to our lives today?

Each of these works has a claim to being not just one of the greatest works in its language and of its time, but one of the greatest ever written in any language at any time. Of all the enduring literary works from the ancient epics through Shakespeare's greatest plays on to the masterpieces of modern literature, including *1984* and *Ulysses*, which came in at numbers 2 and 3, respectively, in the Random House survey, there is no single work of literature more highly regarded than Dante's *Divine Comedy*. Two recent books illustrate different ways a great literary work can remain powerfully relevant and meaningful for readers today.

Prue Shaw's *Reading Dante* does so by raising these questions: What is the relationship between the human and the divine? How did Dante challenge the historical understanding of this relationship? And how do his works continue to challenge our thinking today? Shaw organizes her exploration of Dante's life, world, and work through a series of themes that crosscut among the three parts of his *Commedia* (*Hell*, *Purgatory*, and *Heaven*), and among other works by Dante as well. Dante's (and Shaw's) themes— friendship, power, life, love, time, numbers, and words—take us deeply into the great poem, revealing its relevance for us today. Living with Dante, as Prue Shaw has for half a century, has prepared her to write a book that makes this formidable poet and majestic poem accessible to us, while also making the work understandable, interesting, and engaging.

Another writer has explicated Dante's *Commedia* by relating it directly to his personal life. In his memoir, *In a Dark Wood*, Joseph Luzzi draws on *The Divine Comedy* for insight into his life, which took a tragic turn when his young eight-and-a-half-months pregnant wife was killed in an automobile crash. Within minutes, Luzzi became a widower and father of a baby girl. Raising a daughter with the help of his Sicilian family, his mother most importantly, Luzzi draws heavily on the whole of Dante's religious epic, partly as a way to describe and make palpable his pain and suffering, and partly as an inspiration and model for his journey toward a renewed life of hope, wholeness, and love. Throughout his memoir, Luzzi explains key passages from the *Inferno*, *Purgatorio*, and *Paradiso* as they speak to significant experiences in his life. Like Daniel Mendelsohn working with Homer's *Odyssey*, Joseph Luzzi serves as a critical guide through the *Commedia* and as a self-therapist, using Dante's poem to guide his return to psychic and spiritual health.

Each of these critics celebrates a writer he or she loves. To echo Wordsworth at the end of *The Prelude*—"what we have loved, / Others will love, and we will teach them how" (588).

You Must Change Your Life

Let us consider, finally, two lyric poems, which show us yet other ways literature can affect our lives. James Wright's "A Blessing," is, indeed, what its title suggests, a "blessing," an epiphany even. Once we've considered it from those two standpoints, we will take a turn through Rainer Maria Rilke's sonnet "Archaic Torso of Apollo," in the translation of Stephen Mitchell, the concluding words of which provide the heading above.

James Wright's "A Blessing"

Our word "blessing," which derives from an Old English word meaning "mark as to hallow with blood," is related as well to the French *blesser*, which means "to hurt or to wound." Connotations for "blessing" in later English run in another but not unrelated direction, a blessing being a special kind of gift or grace. The notion of hurt, even pain, hides in our notion of blessing, especially in what James Wright's poem of that title suggests about the experience it describes. The painful aspect of blessing is something akin to the "heavenly hurt," the oxymoronic pleasurable pain described by Christian mystics like Teresa of Avila and depicted in the poems of Richard Crashaw and sculpture of Gianlorenzo Bernini, and later in Emily Dickinson's "There's a certain Slant of light." Wright's poem, however, also embodies the more conventionally understood meaning of blessing, a positive halo that pushes beyond its everyday meaning to deepen into a revelation, in what can only be described as a poem of epiphany.

The original meaning of "epiphany," a sudden awareness of the divine in the ordinary (from *epiphainein* in Greek), has since been secularized to include other kinds of manifestations. James Joyce significantly enlarged the meaning of the term. For Joyce, an epiphany was any sudden, dramatic, or startling moment that seemed to have a heightened significance. In "The Dry Salvages," T. S. Eliot refers to such moments as existing "in and out of time" (*Collected Poems* 199) at "The point of intersection of the timeless / With time" (198); moments, for example, where we "are the music / While the music lasts" (199). Joyce had the idea of collecting such instances of transcendence in a "Book of Epiphanies." He believed it would be a serious task for a man of letters who would exercise extreme care since he would be recording the most delicate and effervescent of experiences.

Poetry has rescued many readers from banal ways of perception; poets have often surprised them into seeing the world in a new way. Some of those poems have led their readers to experience a new reality in which they saw, just for a moment, a world that was unified, expansive, transcendent, sublime.

These special moments are gifts of vision or, in the words of James Wright, blessings, moments in which we might "break into blossom." In the language of Wordsworth, they are times when "we are laid asleep / In body, and become a living soul" ("Tintern Abbey" ll. 45–46). Such moments are flashes of illumination in which the sense of self, the ego, suddenly fades away, and we feel part of something much larger than our sole selves. For Ralph Waldo Emerson, these moments occur in nature. For Virginia Woolf, these "moments of being" can occur anywhere at any time.

Poems of epiphany, like Wright's "A Blessing," are often rich with surprise, astonishment, amazement:

Just off the highway to Rochester, Minnesota,
Twilight bounds softly forth on the grass.
And the eyes of those two Indian ponies
Darken with kindness.
They have come gladly out of the willows
To welcome my friend and me.
We step over the barbed wire into the pasture

Where they have been grazing all day, alone.
They ripple tensely, they can hardly contain their happiness
That we have come.
They bow shyly as wet swans. They love each other.
There is no loneliness like theirs.
At home once more,
They begin munching the young tufts of spring in the
    darkness.
I would like to hold the slenderer one in my arms,
For she has walked over to me
And nuzzled my left hand.
She is black and white,
Her mane falls wild upon her forehead,
And the light breeze moves me to caress her long ear
That is delicate as the skin over a girl's wrist.
Suddenly I realize
That if I stepped out of my body I would break
Into blossom.

The title of Wright's poem perfectly captures its trajectory of
meaning and feeling. The casualness of the poem's opening line
gives no clue to the transcendent experience that awaits its
speaker—and the extraordinary surprises that await the reader as
the poem unfolds. The second line lifts the poem beyond that
matter-of-fact opening, as twilight "bounds softly forth," a shift to
a different semantic register. From there the poem moves quickly
to the Indian ponies, personified with eyes that "Darken with kindness," a phrase made emphatic in one of the poem's shortest lines.
The poet/speaker continues his personification of the ponies, who
are said to come "gladly" to "welcome" the speaker and his friend.
In a mere half dozen lines the poet has established a tone of warmth
and gentleness, setting the stage for a communion between human
and natural worlds, between men and horses.

As the speaker and his friend "step over the barbed wire into the
pasture," they cross a boundary; they enter the world of the ponies,
bringing the animals companionship, whereas before they had
been grazing "alone." The ponies respond to the gesture of the

speaker and his friend: they "ripple" and "bow shyly," which the speaker reads as signs of "love" and "happiness" that help to dispel "loneliness." Grammatically, this "loneliness" refers to the ponies; semantically, by extension, it encompasses the speaker and his friend, who are as eager for physical contact with the ponies as they imagine the ponies are for contact with them.

At this point, Wright's poem swerves, with the speaker's responding to one of the ponies nuzzling his hand with a desire "to hold the slenderer one in [his] arms." He caresses her long ear, which he compares to the soft and delicate skin on a "girl's wrist." As the speaker caresses the slender black-and-white girl-like pony, he has an epiphany, saying: "Suddenly I realize / That if I stepped out of my body I would break / Into blossom."

This realization is expressed in metaphor—of a body blossoming in the manner of a flower fulfilling its *telos*, or final purpose. The poet expresses the speaker's epiphany as a single sentence broken over three lines, two of them short and strongly emphatic. The poem's concluding sentence begins with "Suddenly," a signal that something significant is about to occur. The short line ends with "realize," an indicator of the speaker's understanding. What he realizes is conveyed in the poem's long penultimate line, the meaning of which spills over the word "break," making us pause a moment as we wait for the "blossom" that finishes the sentence and completes the poem's meaning, bringing both the poem and the epiphany it embodies to a consummation.

Rilke's "Archaic Torso of Apollo"

In *Better Living through Criticism*, *New York Times* literary and cultural critic A. O. Scott describes the intersection between literature and life—art and living—through a look at Rainer Maria Rilke's best-known poem, "Archaic Torso of Apollo." Scott analyzes the relationship between Rilke's sonnet and the demands the poem makes upon its readers.

Rilke's poem was inspired by his viewing of an ancient sculpture—a torso of a human figure, an encounter that engaged the poet so powerfully he felt compelled to write "Archaic Torso of Apollo" in response. The poem's most famous line, in translation

actually a half line, "You must change your life," concludes it. These
five monosyllabic words take us by surprise; they bring us up short.
How, we might wonder, does Rilke get to the place where he can
write words that make such a demand on his readers? Here is the
poem in a translation from the German by Stephen Mitchell:

Rainer Maria Rilke

ARCHAIC TORSO OF APOLLO

We cannot know his legendary head
with eyes like ripening fruit. And yet his torso
is still suffused with brilliance from inside,
like a lamp, in which his gaze, now turned to low,

gleams in all its power. Otherwise
the curved breast could not dazzle you so, nor could
a smile run through the placid hips and thighs
to that dark center where procreation flared.

Otherwise this stone would seem defaced
beneath the translucent cascade of the shoulders
and would not glisten like a wild beast's fur:

would not, from all the borders of itself,
burst like a star: for here there is no place
that does not see you. You must change your life.

What does it mean to say that something changes your life? Scott
suggests that it's more than being charmed by the beautiful or ter-
rified by the sublime. We wonder what was different for Rilke before his encounter with the work of art and just how his life changed
after it. And for us readers, how might our lives change in response
to our double encounter, first with Rilke's poem, and second with
the archaic torso of Apollo mediated by it? The ending of Rilke's
poem is as much a command as a revelation, but a revelation and a
command that embody mystery as much as meaning, a mystery
and a meaning that we can only resolve for ourselves.

Scott suggests that Rilke describes not so much the statue itself as what it is like to behold it. Rilke begins with what we don't see: the torso's head and eyes. The torso's partial decomposition and its "archaic" quality—its fragmentary and ancient aspects—put us "in the presence of something that survives from a past beyond our imagining" (67). Paradoxically, once Rilke calls our attention to what's absent, we are mysteriously able "to imagine the invisible" (68). The glowing light of the empty eyes—their ripeness— embodies the life of the intact torso and, even more remarkably, the stone parts that are no longer connected to it. We appreciate the sculpture's incompleteness, Scott suggests, "because of the latent light of those missing eyes, without which we would be looking at nothing but cold, broken stone" (70).

It's eerie.

A second such moment in the poem is expressed in the line "for here there is no place / that does not see you." We experience "the sensation of being suddenly and uncannily visible, exposed, understood" (70). With the shift of pronoun from first to second person, from "we" to "you," the poem itself sees us, fixes us in its gaze. While we are looking at Rilke's poem and at the archaic statue, we are being seen ourselves. Scott writes: "You are opened up, exposed to the universe, which sends you a message through the ventriloquism of ancient marble and modern literature: *You must change your life*" (71).

But just what does this mean? It is not, of course, self-evident. Each of us must interpret the command for ourselves. How, exactly, do we need to change our lives? What kinds of changes are necessary? What kinds of changes are possible? What basis do we have for considering those changes? Does it have something to do with enriching our experience through a more mindful kind of living, through a deeper and more sustained encounter with art, with any or all the arts? To which of art's exhortations must we attend? And how should we do so? What could this mean for us? How badly might we want to find out? And how might we go about discovering answers to these beguiling questions?

CODA Nine Recommended Reading Practices

How should we read to best absorb the benefits reading can offer? The following guidelines should get us going in the right direction. They constitute a reading credo.

> Read actively.
> Read deliberatively.
> Read predictively.
> Read retrospectively.
> Read interpretively.
> Read evaluatively.
> Read purposefully.
> Read habitually.
> Read pleasurably.

Active reading involves close, thoughtful reading in which we make observations, connections, and inferences—reading in which we ask questions about the text. A form of responsive, responsible reading, active reading is serious, even strenuous, requiring, as Thoreau suggests, in *Walden*, the stamina of athletes preparing for Olympic competition.

Deliberative reading is slow, careful reading. As a noun, "deliberation" suggests patient consideration. As a verb, "deliberate" implies the act of thinking, pondering, weighing. As an adjective, "deliberative" connotes purpose, intentionality, leisurely thoughtfulness. In that same chapter on reading in *Walden*, Thoreau advises that "books should be read as deliberately and reservedly as they were written" (403).

Predictive reading highlights our expectations about what's coming based on what we have already encountered in a text. Predictive reading requires imagination; it envisions textual possibilities. In making anticipatory projections as we read, we create expectations the text will gratify or frustrate; in the latter case we revise our predictions or make new ones.

Retrospective reading involves reading backward as well as forward, highlighting reading's essential circularity and spiraling repetition. In tracking back while moving ahead in a text, we make new connections while reevaluating earlier parts of the text in light of later ones. Reading is a cyclical and not a linear experience. It is also recursive. Our expectations are modified, and our memories transformed as we move forward and backward, simultaneously, through a text.

Interpretive reading is analytical reading. In reading interpretively, we seek to understand, construe, and explain a text, first to ourselves and then to others. Interpretation involves actively making meaning, not merely passively absorbing it. Interpretation depends on inference. Requiring both intellectual comprehension and emotional apprehension, interpretation is built on inferences, without which there is no interpretation at all.

Evaluative reading requires a consideration of both a work's *value*—how highly we esteem it—and its *values*, particularly its social, cultural, and moral dispositions. A work's value will be in direct proportion to how much it invites our attention, how strongly it affects our feelings, how effectively it instructs us, and how powerfully it engages us. We value different works for different reasons. And we value the same work differently at different times in our lives.

Purposeful reading requires reading intentionally—for engagement, intellectual development, solace, and companionship. We are social creatures at our core, and reading provides ways into the profound pleasures and value this kind of human connection affords. Purposeful reading can sharpen our powers of discernment, increase our literary tact, deepen our judgment, and lead us to wisdom.

Habitual reading. Reading well—both confidently and competently—is best accomplished through regular, daily reading. Making reading a regular part of our day testifies to its importance for our intellectual, emotional, and psychic well-being. Through habitual reading we develop a level of reading comfort essential for long-term reading success and pleasure.

Pleasurable reading. We should seek and take pleasure from our reading. We should read books and articles we like to read and that we look forward to reading. When we read books that interest us, we learn from them, and we allow them to work their magic on us. Reading for pleasure solidifies and intensifies the habit of reading.

To read well we need to read with intellectual and emotional engagement—actively and deliberatively; predictively and retrospectively; interpretively and evaluatively; purposefully, habitually and pleasurably. These reading practices pay countless dividends and offer multiple, lifelong reading pleasures. They can change our lives.

PRINT AND DIGITAL READING

Books allow you to fully explore a topic and immerse yourself in a deeper way than most media.
—MARK ZUCKERBERG.

As with any new technology, new reading technologies coexist with older ones. For example, though we no longer typically read texts in the form of scrolls, their reading persists for religious purposes, with the Torah preserved in Hebrew on scrolls used in Jewish ritual, notable in the tradition of the bar and bat mitzvah. And, of course, we "scroll" through text on our smartphones, tablets, and computers.

We continue to listen to radio, watch television, and view movies in theaters, although streaming video on phones and tablets has become ubiquitous, especially now in the time of Covid-19. So too, it can be argued, we will continue to have bound books even as e-books become increasingly available. Recent statistics suggest that e-book consumption is slowing and print book reading regaining some of its previously lost ground.

That being said, however, reading in print differs from reading online; reading books and magazines in print is not the same experience as reading them in an electronically transmitted, digitized format. What are some of these differences? What are their implications for different kinds of reading? And, further, what does the increasing move to digital reading portend for the next generation of readers? In what manner and how well will those readers read works of literature especially?

In a *New York Times* op-ed piece, Verlyn Klinkenborg, who acknowledges having read hundreds of books on his tablet, suggests that the e-books he reads disappear not just into cyberspace but from his vision and memory as well. As a result, the physicality and the attendant substantiality of those books are effaced. He notes that registering the size, heft, and shape of physical books, their typography and page layout, helps him remember that he has indeed read those books. He is more likely to forget the e-books he reads; without physical books to look at and hold, he is not reminded of having read them. Klinkenborg admits that both e-books and physical books "stir us into reverie"; they "revise our consciousness," as they entertain, inform, and even change us. But e-books make reading even more ephemeral than the reading of print books, whose physical presence testifies to their having been read, and whose bound presence substantiates the imaginative act of reading. Sven Birkerts writes that just looking at his books gives him a sense of "expectant tranquility" and a "sense of futurity" (cited in Giraldi 410), as he anticipates and imagines the pleasures to come.

In sync with Klinkenborg and Birkerts, Joseph Epstein, in "The Bookish Life," suggests that "print has more weight, a more substantial feel, makes a greater demand on one's attention, than the pixel." Epstein claims that readers attend to style more carefully in printed texts than in pixelated ones. He, himself, skips and skims when reading digital texts, something he doesn't do when reading books in print. Epstein recommends segregating digital and print reading, with "pixels for information and convenience" and "print for knowledge and pleasure." It's not that one medium is necessarily better than the other; it's simply that they differ significantly enough to be reserved for different types of reading and different reading purposes. That's the first point to emphasize.

And so, for example, a screen is less than ideal for reading a book of significant length. We tire faster from screen reading. And we are more easily distracted. We lose our place more readily and find it with greater difficulty. Digitized words disappear off the screen, replaced by others, which similarly evaporate.

Second, recent research suggests that we retain information better and comprehend texts more completely when we read them in print. Neurological studies suggest that we read print books more comprehensively, partly because of the tactile and sensuous nature of the experience, and partly because of its aesthetic quality.

We remember more and we remember better when we read print rather than pixels (Giraldi 44).

A third research finding suggests that we engage with printed text more fully and are more likely to become "lost" in a writer's fictional world when reading about that world in a printed book. William Gass has noted that screen-read books have no substance to them, "no materiality" (33). Franklin Foer describes his need to retreat to the silent world of the printed page, which he can rub between his fingers, and which is not surveilled in the ways digitized texts are. The print book, read in a silent personal space, is unlinked, disconnected, free of interruption and distraction.

In *The Rise and Fall of the Bible* Timothy Beal considers how the impact of the digital revolution and the end of the dominance of print culture will change the meaning of the word and the idea of the book. Beal describes three dimensions of reading—hypertextual, processual, and collaborative (189). The most frequently discussed of these is hypertextuality, the fact that any text can be linked to a multitude of other texts and images. One result of these extensive linkages is the proliferative nature of texts as they flow and overflow into one another, blurring the line between text and context. Beal's processual notion suggests how texts exist in complex networked relationships with other texts. They are, thus, always in the process of being formed and re-formed. And thus a third significant difference between print and digital reading is that print books are stable in ways that digital books are not.

A fourth point, and a serious concern of researchers who investigate readers' brains, is that digital reading differs so much from reading in print that readers' brains are being altered in ways we do not yet understand. In *Reading in the Brain*, Stanislas Dehaene investigates the cognitive neuroscience of language in the brain. He examines brain-imaging studies, with an emphasis on the prefrontal cortex, and how it develops neurological pathways conducive to learning to read. Maryanne Wolf, in *Proust and the Squid* explores the history of human reading, explains human intellectual development conjoined with reading, and describes the science behind impediments to learning to read (4). Her recent *Reader, Come Home*, subtitled *The Reading Brain in a Digital World*, carries forward her argument that the "act of learning to read added an entirely new circuit to our hominid brain's repertoire" and "rewired the brain, which transformed the nature of human thought" (2). Wolf turns her attention to how reading has changed in our current digital world. She suggests that science and technology can explain the "impact of different forms of reading on cognition and culture," and how that understanding can help change "the reading circuits" of the next generation of readers, those immersed in digital reading today (4). These sanguine aims exude both hope and optimism for the future of reading both digitally and in print.

In *Reader, Come Home,* Wolf considers the implications for the reading brains of children growing up in a digital world. She suggests that with the dramatic upsurge in digital information processing, both children and adults experience increasing levels of distraction and fragmented attention, accompanied by a desire for fast searches for information and an impatience with deep cognitive abilities. The result is a lack of "cognitive patience." With an escalation in the volume and tempo of visual stimuli via digitization comes an inevitable decrease in the amount of time available to process, analyze, and evaluate information, and a decreased ability to connect it to what we know (122).

Consequently, deep reading, the kind of slow, patient, thoughtful consideration of texts necessary for long-lasting learning, is at risk. Wolf sounds a warning: during the past decade we have changed considerably "*how much* we read, *how* we read, *what* we read, and *why* we read, with a 'digital chain' that connects the links among them all and extracts a tax we have only begun to tally" (her italics; 72). These developments, she contends, are affecting the maturing brains of young readers, with a loss in digital readers' ability to do the kind of deep reading associated with reading serious books, literature included, in print. It's a loss that evokes cries of despair from novelist John Fowles, who believes that it would take an ecological disaster or some other form of catastrophe to return the majority of people to reading (67). The coronavirus pandemic is, possibly, one such event.

The questions Wolf poses to her readers, directly, while confessing to the atrophy of her own ability to do the kind of deep reading she grew up with, are worth quoting in their entirety (in my bulleted formatting):

- Do you, my reader, read with less attention and perhaps even less memory for what you have read?
- Do you notice when reading on a screen that you are increasingly reading for key words and skimming over the rest?
- Has this habit or style of screen reading bled over to your reading of hard copy?
- Do you find yourself reading the same passage over and over to understand its meaning? (96)

Along with Wolf's questions I would ask whether you have stopped reading long works, big books, difficult books—whether you have, perhaps, stopped reading novels or historical works or whatever it is you spent deep time immersed in a few years ago, but no longer seem to have the time, energy, patience, or perseverance to read today.

Here are a few more of Wolf's questions, again with my bullets:

- Have you become so inured to quick précis of information that you no longer feel the need or possess the time for your own analysis of this information?
- Do you find yourself gradually avoiding denser, more complex analyses, even those that are readily available?
- Are you less able to find the same enveloping pleasure you once derived from your former reading self?
- What if, one day, you pause and wonder if you yourself are truly changing and, worst of all, do not have the time to do a thing about it? (96)

It's the last of this set of questions that I find most discouraging. I would amend that one to focus less on lack of time and more on a diminished inclination to do anything about it—perhaps because the value of deep reading seems to be fading overall in society, in academic life as well as in professional life, to say nothing of our personal lives.

I share the alarm Wolf sounds about the ways digital reading erodes the kinds of deep, sustained reading necessary for understanding and for critical and creative thinking. Like some of the other writers quoted earlier, I believe the habits reading books in print encourages need to be preserved in the shift to digital reading among the young. And especially for reading literature.

Not everyone agrees, of course.

In "Reader, I Googled It," a *New Yorker* review of Leah Price's *What We Talk about When We Talk about Books*, Dan Chiasson celebrates the author's embrace of a wide range of reading practices, formats, and experiences. Like Wolf, Price recognizes that digital reading is here to stay as the dominant form of reading for many people, millennials and other younger readers especially. She also reminds us that print was once a destabilizing technology, Socrates being perhaps the best-known alarmist about its dangers, especially the erosion of memory.

Chiasson raises some important questions about reading, while noting that even those who read printed books tend to have conversations about them online, with the internet working synergistically with print reading to invigorate our current talk about reading—whether we read primarily off- or online, with print or digital texts. He also suggests that the internet serves as a motivational impulse for reading, and that publisher and bookseller websites, along with chat rooms and major internet providers, players, and purveyors, collectively, advance the cause of reading, including the reading of serious books in both print and digital form. That's one of the benefits of digital reading.

Chiasson suggests that particular benefits accrue to reading nonfiction online, largely in enabling readers to take advantage of hyperlinks. He sees value in reading biography this way, especially, as a reader can readily link to various forms of contextual information—in particular, historical background and other connections with biographical figures with a role in the biography being read. This makes a degree of sense, for sure. And yet I can't help thinking that in reading Boswell's *Life of Johnson* digitally, I would be torn between focusing on Boswell's literary artistry in dramatizing Johnson and his circle, and the centrifugal pull to look up information, including images, of the various characters who figure in Boswell's account of Johnson's life. It would be a little like trying to read Boswell's biography while simultaneously diving into Leo Damrosch's *The Club*, which discusses Johnson and Boswell in relation to the lives and work of Edward Gibbon, David Garrick, Edmund Burke, Oliver Goldsmith, Richard Brinsley Sheridan, Sir Joshua Reynolds, Hester Thrale, and David Hume, toggling back and forth between his book and Boswell's biography. Such a way of reading has a number of virtues, clearly, but appreciating Boswell's literary-biographical accomplishment isn't one of them. Zigzagging between a literary achievement like Boswell's *Life of Johnson* and a vast array of social, cultural, and historical materials bifurcates attention. My own preference is to read Boswell's book alone, and either before or after to read a book such as Damrosch's *The Club* by itself, giving each my full attention. Others may prefer to do just the opposite. Whichever reading practice we might pursue in this or other similar instances, we are reading differently, for sure.

More than a decade ago, N. Katherine Hayles published a provocative article in the *ADE Bulletin* entitled "How We Read: Close, Hyper, Machine." I forgo discussion of her third category, machine reading, here, to focus on the print/digital divide. Hayles identifies a pair of related crucial challenges, which have still not been adequately addressed: (1) how to convert digital reading into improved reading ability; (2) how to bridge the gap between digital and print literacy. Hayles notes that these two types of reading run parallel, without transfer between them. She is not the only one to note the numerous differences that separate print and digital reading. But she offers what is perhaps the most thorough description of the two types of reading.

Hayles describes digital reading essentially as "hyperreading," which includes skimming texts, scanning them, "pecking" or hyperlinking texts, as well as pulling out a few items from long texts, and "juxtaposing," or reading across texts with multiple computer windows open. She relates these hyperreading practices to those involved in archival research, which, like hyperreading, requires reading strategies different from those needed for close reading or deep reading.

This, of course, makes perfect sense. I would add two things, however. First, that the kind of hyperreading behaviors Hayles describes can also be used when one is reading printed texts—and not only during archival research, but in the process of doing any kind of research among books, journals, magazines, advertisements, pamphlets, brochures, broadsides, flyers, and other print media. Second, that the skimming and scanning functions of hyperreading have been long known, practiced, and taught in books and courses for "basic" readers. Books introducing students to the elements of college reading—learning to negotiate their way through college introductory textbooks, for example—are replete with strategies and exercises on skimming and scanning. There is nothing new here. What's different about hyperreading is that multiple texts are open simultaneously. And there's a further difference that Hayles doesn't mention: the dangerous seductions of distraction, not by the texts open for research, but by those available at the click of a mouse that have nothing to do with the reading project undertaken—the distractions of web browsing and internet shopping, for instance, along with the profusion of seductive clickbait.

Hayles cites Nicholas Carr's *The Shallows*, in which the author claims that web reading (Hayles's hyperreading) leads to a diminished capacity for deep reading. Carr argues that web hyperreading decreases one's ability to focus and to concentrate for sustained periods, resulting in shallow thinking. He argues, further, that internet reading differs significantly from book reading; a screen, he contends, is not a page.

Think, for example, of the kinds of reading you do online as compared with the reading you do in books. Think about your own reading process in these different reading environments. Consider the extent to which there is overlap—some aspects of the process seem quite similar, while others differ dramatically, particularly a tendency, when reading online, to follow links, to break away from one page of text to visit linked sites, or to break from the electronic page to respond to email and Facebook updates. Or consider how scrolling up and down electronic pages differs from flipping pages in a book. Many e-book readers now mimic certain actual book features, notably the turning of pages with a flip of the finger.

These observations about reading, however, suggest only minimally what is at stake in our use of the continually evolving electronic technologies for the ways we *think* and process information. When we turn on our computers, we are entering "an ecosystem of interruption technologies" (cited in Carr 91), one that shortens our attention spans, limits our ability to focus and think deeply, and, over time, actually rewires the neurons in our brains to make us intellectual jugglers rather than deep thinkers. The frequent interruptions we experience while using our electronic devices—email notifications, Twitter and Facebook updates, ubiquitous advertisements, page crawls, and the like—scatter our thoughts, dilute our concentration, and increase our level of anxiety.

There is no question that the two types of reading—digital and print—are necessary and valuable. Hypertextual, linked reading is useful for gaining a quick overview of material and for switching among multiple texts. Deep attention, focused reading is necessary for understanding complex works of literature, music, math, science, and more. It's not that one kind of reading is good and the other bad, but rather that each caters to different reading and thinking purposes. For much of the academic work students do in college and for some of their subsequent professional work, they need skills associated with the sustained reading of serious texts in print. Hypertext reading will not provide them with those deeper reading and thinking skills.

Students must learn to do both kinds of reading well. The problem today, however, is that they do much more reading in hypertext mode than they do in a deep sustained way—whether they read texts online or in print. Hales quotes Maryanne Wolf's *Proust and the Squid* to the effect that we need to teach students to become "bitextual or multitextual, able to analyze texts flexibly in different ways, with more deliberate instruction at every stage of development on the inferential, demanding aspects of any text" (226). This represents the goal, the ideal. But what's the best way to reach that goal, to achieve that ideal? That remains an open question.

Hayles recognizes the importance of detecting patterns for both kinds of reading. This, certainly, is a supremely valuable skill for all kinds of reading across academic disciplines. And yet to detect patterns is not enough. That's a basic skill, one that follows from making observations. It's a matter of making connections among observations, detecting relationships, establishing patterns. Those two related reading skills are foundational, critically important for reading texts both online and in print. But students need to learn how to move from those foundational reading skills to making inferences, and then from making inferences to drawing provisional conclusions in the form of interpretations, interpretations that can be supported with textual evidence and logical reasoning. Hyperreading does not encourage these more reflective critical reading and thinking skills.

Wolf emphasizes the importance of making inferences; she values textual analysis, which has long been the purview of close reading, careful attentive reading—the kind of reading associated with reading books, especially with the reading of serious books in all fields, and usually in print. Unfortunately, what students gain with their hyperreading is not nearly as important as what they are losing with their retreat from the deep, sustained attention of analytical, interpretive reading.

That kind of reading, I believe, is what students, and all readers, generally, need to continue doing; or to learn how to do if they have not yet made much progress in that type of reading proficiency. "Digital discernment," as Kiersten Greene has noted (182), is a laudable goal—learning to read digital texts critically. And Greene has created a set of strategies to help her students (largely graduate students preparing for teaching careers) become digital critical readers. Among them are a template she designed for reading a website critically and techniques for the digital annotation of texts. Her article "Text(ured) Considerations" lays out the details of these practices. And yet, even so, I fear that an overindulgence in digital reading may undermine the kinds of critical reading needed most for understanding and evaluating information disseminated and arguments advanced through various forms of social media via digital technologies. Digital discernment may be undermined by the nature of the digital medium in which readers, especially student readers, are immersed.

In "A Shared Horizon: Critical Reading and Digital Natives," my NYU colleague Anton Borst captures the fears of many teachers worried about the future of students' learning when their first source of information is Google rather than the library, and their primary path to information is through their smartphones (49). He embraces Hayles's and Wolf's hope that we can help students learn to apply their critical reading skills, whatever they may be, to the newest technologies. Borst demonstrates how to teach students to make critical judgments about internet sources and to evaluate information they consume through digital media. He begins by having them reflect on their use of digital media, and how those media shape their learning. Borst helps his students cultivate "self-reflective learning," an essential first step toward their gaining at least a modicum of control of the digital platforms, products, and programs they use to consume information and develop their understanding of what they read.

One engaging approach to helping students develop their critical reading and research skills is provided by Amy Hamlin of Saint Catherine University in "Approaching Intellectual Emancipation: Critical Reading in Art, Art History, and Wikipedia." Hamlin has her students participate in a Wikipedia edit-a-thon as a culminating activity in her Women in Art course. Her students research a neglected woman artist and contribute a new entry to Wikipedia. Required to read Wikipedia critically for its representation of gender in the arts, they craft a critical appraisal of their chosen artist to counter the sexism endemic in online environments like Wikipedia. To do this work productively, students are guided by their teacher in a series of critical reading exercises of Wikipedia articles on women artists. That critical reading of the website lays the groundwork for their deeper research, and for their opportunity to highlight the accomplishments of women artists and identify their cultural significance and impact. Hamlin's Wikipedia edit-a-thon project provides an exemplary model for critical textual engagement. In their work on Wikipedia, her students consider message and media; in doing so, they develop an awareness of Wikipedia's limits in achieving its stated aim: to make *all* knowledge freely available for *all* people through open, collective design and development.

Conclusion

In *Reading and the Reader*, Philip Davis expresses a concern with how literature deepens and extends thought, yielding "more than its writers know" (4). His book is about epistemology—what literature knows and how literature knows, and how literature helps readers discover "thoughts that otherwise may be personally unavailable to them or that go unrecognized and undervalued" (ix). In his excursion into literary knowing, Davis provides a guide to the growth of the reader's mind.

Sven Birkerts laments a loss of focus, attention, and concentration among readers, students in particular, that has increased exponentially over the past quarter century. In a preface to the second edition of his *Gutenberg Elegies*, he describes "a deep transformation in the nature of reading . . . from focused, sequential, text-centered engagement to a far more lateral kind of encounter" (xiv). It's a textual encounter, I might add, that has become ever more fragmented, shattering readers' concentration and scattering their attention. Distracted readers present an increasingly problematic challenge today for teachers at every educational level.

What I have tried to provide throughout *You Are What You Read* are ways to engage productively with texts, especially works of literature, whether digitized or in print. Throughout, I offer suggestions for how to deepen textual understanding and enhance readerly pleasure in textual encounters. I echo Rebecca Solnit's thinking as she reminds us that reading writing that is worth the effort requires "slowness and thoughtfulness" and heightened attention so we can "explore what language can do to give us joy," and along the way "sharpen our perception and deepen our awareness" (Introduction xxvii).

I sincerely hope that the ways in to texts I explore, and the approaches to conscientious, reflective reading I describe, prove useful for readers of this book and for those helping others learn to read more efficaciously—in both print and digital formats. Much is at stake for the quality of our thinking and for the breadth and depth of our learning. And much is at stake, as well, I believe, for the quality of our living. Reading well may be a luxury, but it is one that can enrich our lives immeasurably.

WHAT TO READ AND WHY

After reading a new book, never allow yourself another new one till you have read an old one in between.
—C. S. LEWIS

What We Read

What literature should we read? And why? Large questions, surely, and answerable only with guaranteed disagreements evident as soon as any claims are made for what is worth reading. Nonetheless, I here venture into that contentious territory.

Henry David Thoreau in his masterpiece *Walden* suggests that we should read the best books first—or we may not have time to read them at all. But what is the best and the greatest literature that Thoreau, among others, recommends? What literary works that writers invested their lives in making should we read, and read them, as Thoreau suggests, "as deliberately and reservedly as they were written" (403)?

First, the book of Genesis in the Bible. All fifty chapters, including the story of Creation (actually two creation stories spliced together), the story of the great Flood and Noah's Ark, Cain and Abel, Jacob and Esau, and the masterful novella of sibling rivalry, ingenuity, and morality, Joseph and his brothers, which concludes this first biblical book. Included in the Genesis stories are some of the Bible's most fascinating female characters, beginning, of course, with Eve, and including Sarah, Rachel, Tamar, and Rebecca. There is much more great literature in the Hebrew and Christian scriptures—Job and Ecclesiastes, Psalms and Proverbs, Ruth and Esther, Samuel and Kings, the Gospels and Revelation.

Second, Homer's magisterial, influential epics, the *Iliad* and the *Odyssey*. The *Iliad* is the story of the Trojan War, with the Greeks battling the Trojans in their home city of Troy. The emphasis of this epic is on the violence of war and on the wrath of the greatest warrior ever, Achilles, a pure killing machine. But in the work's final "books" or sections, Homer shows a different side of Achilles, a more humane and compassionate side, which is revealed in some of the most remarkable and moving scenes in any literature.

So, too, with the *Odyssey*, the story of Odysseus, known also by his Latin name, Ulysses. You may remember the fabulous adventure episodes from the *Odyssey*, most famously, perhaps, Odysseus's encounter with the giant one-eyed Cyclops. But those great adventure sequences do not contain the whole story—or even its most important parts, which include, instead, the episodes about Odysseus's son, Telemachus, and his wife, Penelope, one of the great heroines in all of literature, and a worthy spousal match for and equal of the heroic Odysseus. The final section of the *Odyssey*, including Odysseus's homecoming and reunion with his son, their slaughter of the suitors, and the hero's reunion with Penelope, are justly famous.

Nor should we overlook the great Roman epic, Virgil's *Aeneid*, which echoes both the *Iliad* and the *Odyssey* in many ways. In book 2 of the *Aeneid* you will find what you cannot find in Homer: the famous story of the Trojan Horse, how the Greeks tricked the Trojans into letting a giant wooden horse filled with Greek warriors inside the locked gates of Troy—and what happens as a result. In book 4 of the *Aeneid* you will find the story of Dido and Aeneas, one of the world's most unforgettable tragic love stories.

Strongly influenced by Virgil, medieval Italian poet Dante Alighieri, whose *Divine Comedy* is among the supreme achievements of the literary imagination, divides the work into three parts:

- *Inferno* (hell)
- *Purgatorio* (purgatory)
- and *Paradiso* (heaven).

These are the three places in medieval theology where the soul can be sent after death. One of the most striking features of the *Inferno* is the law of symbolic retribution, in which the punishment is appropriate to the sin. Murderers are punished by being immersed in a river of boiling blood; the depth of their immersion corresponds to the degree of their bloody violence in life. Gluttons are punished by being made to lie in the filthy slush of decayed garbage. Lust and anger are punished in the upper portion of hell, where the punishments are less painful. Violence and deceit are punished in hell's deeper recesses.

Because fraud and treachery are, for Dante, the worst of sins, these are punished at the very bottom of hell. Dante's scheme is so carefully worked out that he divides the betrayers into categories— betrayers of kin, of country, of guests and hosts, and, finally, those who betrayed their masters. Betrayal is the worst sin of all for Dante. He represents it with the following examples: Brutus and Cassius, who betrayed their emperor, Julius Caesar; Judas Iscariot, who betrayed Jesus; Satan, who betrayed God.

A vivid description of the *Inferno* is provided by Dianne Hales in *La Bella Lingua*, where she mentions that Dante the pilgrim narrator "meets thirty monsters, takes two hair-raising boat rides, faints twice, and witnesses the damned being whipped, bitten, crucified, burned, butchered, deformed by repulsive diseases, transformed into shrubs and snakes, buried alive in flaming graves, skewered into rocky ground, frozen in the ice, and immersed in mud, excrement, boiling blood, or pitch" (64).

Other medieval narrative and epic poems are worth reading, as well. The greatest of the Anglo-Saxon epics is *Beowulf*. Although the work was composed in the early eighth century, the only surviving manuscript dates from the tenth. *Beowulf* is a largely Germanic tale. It is set in Denmark, and its action exemplifies the values of a warrior society. King Beowulf is referred to as "ring giver," and "dispenser of treasure." His duty is to take care of his loyal thanes, or noblemen. The act of giving has a spiritual side; out of generosity, unity and brotherhood emerge. This bonding, called *comitatus*, is balanced by the threat of death.

There are hints of a Christian perspective in *Beowulf*, although these hints are supplied by the narrator, rather than by the characters. Beowulf's funeral is entirely pagan as is his immortality—the celebration of his memory in the poem itself that recounts his exploits. In contrast to *Beowulf*, the short lyric poem, "Caedmon's Hymn," the oldest extant English poem, from around 675, employs the language of Anglo-Saxon heroic verse in an explicitly Christian context. Like a heroic king, God is referred to as the *Weard*, or Guardian, of his kingdom.

The Song of Roland is one of the most famous literary works of medieval France. It is a *chanson de geste*, or song of deeds, dating from the mid-eleventh century. A long stanzaic poem, it consists of more than four thousand lines. *The Song of Roland* is based on a historical incident from the year 778. It tells the story of the Christian army of Charlemagne doing battle against the Muslim Saracens. The poem is noted for the clarity and elegance of its language, the simplicity of its narrative, and the precision of its detail. The feudal code of honor serves as a foundation for and a standard against which to measure the actions of its characters.

One last Western epic on your list should be *Paradise Lost*, by the seventeenth-century English writer John Milton. Not to be missed are the first two books, which describe Satan and his minions, who were cast into hell, where they hold council on how to seek revenge against God. You might read, also, books 4 and 9, which detail the story of Adam and Eve in the Garden of Eden, their temptation, their fall, and their loss of paradise. The conclusion of the poem in book 12 shows Adam and Eve, hand in hand, leaving the Garden of Eden and going forth into the world to confront the challenges that await them. Read Milton's epic for its majestic language, its broad and deep learning, and its successful attempt, as Milton put it, "to justify the ways of God to man."

Nor should we forget or omit the earliest, most ancient, of all literary works that have been preserved, the *Epic of Gilgamesh*. This renowned work of world literature exists in a number of ancient languages and scripts, including that of the ancient Sumerians and Babylonians. *Gilgamesh* explores the themes of friendship, of mortality and the search for immortality, as well as the relationship between men and their gods. It is the oldest extant exploration of these eternal questions in literary form.

Epics from Asian traditions worth reading include the *Mahabharata* and the *Ramayana* from India. These two critically important works can be compared, respectively, to Homer's *Iliad* and *Odyssey*. The *Mahabharata* was composed over a period of eight hundred years—between 400 BCE. and 400 CE. It chronicles the story of a pair of rival warring families, and emphasizes their battles and their warrior culture, somewhat as Homer's *Iliad* chronicles the Trojan War. The *Mahabharata*, though, is a more philosophical work than the *Iliad*, as it includes an important source of Hindu spiritual teaching, the Bhagavad Gita. The Gita explores the moral conflict experienced by Arjuna, a warrior who struggles with his duty to kill his kinsmen. When Arjuna sees his relatives ready to kill one another, he puts down his weapons and refuses to fight. His charioteer, Krishna, an avatar of the god Vishnu, tells Arjuna that it is his duty to fight. Arjuna learns that the spirit in which an act is performed is what matters most; because he fights to fulfill his duty as a member of the Kshatriyas, the warrior class, his behavior is irreproachable.

The oldest Hindu epic, the *Ramayana* (The Way of Rama), was composed by Valmiki in the sixth century BCE. Its narrative origins lie in Indian folk traditions a century earlier. Much like Homer, Valmiki gathered the various strands of the story into a cohesive work of literature. Like the *Odyssey*, the *Ramayana* focuses on a marital relationship, in this case between Prince Rama and his faithful wife, Sita. Also, like Homer's *Odyssey*, the Indian epic uses myths, legends, and moral tales to convey social, moral, and ethical values. Its hero, Prince Rama, models the behavior of the ideal son, brother, husband, warrior, and king. Sita loves, honors, and serves her husband with absolute fidelity, much like Odysseus's wife, Penelope. Husband and wife govern their lives by truth (*dharma*) rather than self-interest, and thus stand as models of Hindu life.

Among the most important African epics are the *Epic of Son-Jara* and *Sundiata: An Epic of Old Mali*. These ancient narratives record the exploits of cultural heroes who blur the lines separating human, deity, animal, ancestor, and spirit. As in the epic literature of Greece and Rome, India and Sumeria, African epics transmit values of immense cultural importance. *Sundiata*, named for the founder of the Mali Empire, tells the story of this hero's rise to power and eventual defeat of his enemy Soumaora at the Battle of Krina in 1230 CE. The epic was not written down until the twentieth century, first in French and later translated into English.

The great work of Mayan myth and literature is the *Popol Vuh*, an epic narrative that describes the creation of the world. Written in the K'iche' language around 1500, but regarded as having been extant during the Mayan classic era, the *Popol Vuh* outlines traditional Mayan views on human beings as well as the origins of the world. According to the story, the gods wished to create intelligent beings who would praise them. They made three unsuccessful attempts, using mud, wood, and animals as materials, before they decided to use water and maize, critically important substances in Mesoamerican culture. As do the Homeric epics for ancient Greece and the *Mahabharata* for ancient India, the *Popol Vuh* serves Mesoamerica as a repository of its most important cultural ideals and values.

Epics are very likely not among your everyday reading fare. Some of the books you read in various genres are easy to enjoy, are interesting and accessible, and quite simply just plain fun to read. We don't demand too much from this kind of literature, and we shouldn't. But we also shouldn't expect these books to give us the bigger payoff of serious literature, including epics.

So we might enjoy a balanced diet including lighter literary fare, popular fiction, perhaps, the kind of books you might read on a plane or at the beach. But we can also experience the joys of reading deeper, more probing and demanding books. In addition to the kinds of works already mentioned, there are numerous wonderful novels, beginning with those written in the eighteenth century—which by some accounts saw the rise of the novel form—through the many outstanding novels written since then.

Much, but not all, of the literature in this second category might be considered "classics," literary works that have stood the perennial test of time, that have lasted through the years, decades, and centuries because they continue to have something of interest and importance to say to us. Of earlier novels, we might read Defoe's *Robinson Crusoe*, *Moll Flanders*, and *Journal of the Plague Year*, Fielding's *Tom Jones* and *Joseph Andrews*; of those in the next century,

Austen's *Emma* and *Pride and Prejudice*, Eliot's *Middlemarch*, Dickens's *Great Expectations* and *Bleak House*, Brontë's *Jane Eyre*; in the same century but across the ocean, the already-mentioned Melville's *Moby-Dick* and James's *The Portrait of a Lady*, Hawthorne's *The Scarlet Letter*, Twain's *Adventures of Huckleberry Finn*; and, not to be forgotten, the great Russian novels that include Tolstoy's *Anna Karenina* and *War and Peace*, along with Dostoyevsky's *Crime and Punishment* and *The Brothers Karamazov.*

This little list should include great French novels, such as Flaubert's *Madame Bovary*, Balzac's *Père Goriot*, German- and Spanish-language fiction, including Goethe's *Sorrows of Young Werther* and the much older *Don Quixote* by Cervantes. Also included should be Joseph Conrad's *Heart of Darkness* and *Lord Jim*, and the splendid fiction of South American writers, such as Machado de Assis and his wondrous *Posthumous Memoirs of Brás Cubas*, Borges and Cortázar, whose *Ficciones* and *Hopscotch*, respectively, present alternative worlds, as do the novels of Isabel Allende and Gabriel García Márquez, with their *House of the Spirits* and *One Hundred Years of Solitude*, with which we get ourselves to the twentieth century.

But let's backtrack for a closer look at *Don Quixote* (c. 1615), which some consider the world's first novel, and at another work sometimes awarded that honor: the medieval epic-length Japanese narrative *The Tale of Genji* (c. 1010).

Don Quixote is among the most influential books of the Western world. Its eponymous hero has given his name to our English word "quixotic," which means impulsive and impractically chivalrous in the manner of the "knight of the woeful countenance," Don Quixote himself. The greatest of all picaresque novels, or novels of the road, *Don Quixote*, was composed between 1603 and 1615. The work's central character, Don Quixote de la Mancha, wants more than anything to become a "knight errant," the kind of hero he has read about in books. The knight errant traveled around saving ladies from danger and defeating dragons in single combat. In fact, though, Don Quixote is at once noble and buffoonish. What he imagines and what is real are two very different things. His horse, which he envisions as a noble steed, is really all skin and bones. His companion, Sancho Panza, whom he calls his squire, is a peasant boy. His lady Dulcinea is a stablewoman unaware of his love and devotion. And the giants he imagines fighting with his lance are nothing but windmills.

A much earlier book with a claim to being the first novel was written by Murasaki Shikibu (c. 976–c. 1026), a member of the Japanese aristocracy. Her *The Tale of Genji* is a sprawling narrative of court life, spanning many generations. It features the hero, Prince Genji, among a host of characters, including many women who share his love. The work is highly regarded for its psychological subtlety and its rich portrayal of character. It reveals a great deal about the refined court life during Japan's elegant Heian period (794–1185).

Coming back once again to the twentieth century, we find many splendid works of fiction by writers the world over, whose books provide the deepest literary and thinking pleasures. Fiction by Thomas Mann (*Death in Venice* and *The Magic Mountain*), Franz Kafka ("The Metamorphosis," *The Trial*, and *The Castle*), Marcel Proust (*Remembrance of Things Past*), James Joyce (*Dubliners, Portrait of the Artist, Ulysses*), and Virginia Woolf (*Mrs. Dalloway* and *To the Lighthouse*); novels by Ernest Hemingway: *The Sun Also Rises* and *A Farewell to Arms* and William Faulkner: *The Sound and the Fury* and *As I Lay Dying*, along with F. Scott Fitzgerald's *The Great Gatsby*. Not to be missed is fiction by Aldous Huxley (*Brave New World* and *Brave New World Revisited*) and George Orwell (*Animal Farm* and *1984*); E. M. Forster (*Howard's End* and *A Passage to India*) and D. H. Lawrence (*Women in Love* and *The Collected Short Stories*); short stories by Eudora Welty and Katherine Anne Porter and Flannery O'Connor; fiction both long and short by James Baldwin and Ralph Ellison (*Invisible Man*) and Toni Morrison (*Beloved* and *Song of Solomon*); by Saul Bellow (*Herzog* and *The Adventures of Augie March*) and Bernard Malamud (*The Natural, The Fixer*) and Philip Roth (*Goodbye Columbus, American Pastoral, The Human Stain*), and fiction of the early twenty-first century, including works by the Nobel laureate J. M. Coetzee (*Disgrace, The Life and Times of Michael K, Waiting for the Barbarians*) and the twice-honored Booker Prize winner Hilary Mantel (*Wolf Hall, Bring Up the Bodies,* and *The Mirror and the Light*). And this list of stellar fiction should include Canadian novelists like

Margaret Atwood (*The Handmaid's Tale* and *The Testament*), Mordecai Richler (*Barney's Version*), Carol Fields (*The Stone Diaries*), and the Nobel Prize–winning short story writer Alice Munro (*Dear Life* and *Carried Away*).

Among the many other writers and books worth reading are the contemporary fiction writers Chimamanda Ngozi Adichie, Aravind Adiga, Julian Barnes, Peter Carey, Ta-Nehisi Coates, Junot Diaz, Louise Erdrich, Elena Ferrante, Mary Gaitskill, Kazuo Ishiguro, Karl Ove Knausgaard, Cormac McCarthy, Ian McEwan, Haraki Murakami, Richard Powers, Marilynne Robinson, Arundhati Roy, Zadie Smith, Colm Tóibín, and many, many more.

And then there are the dramatists. Heading the list are plays by the ancient Greeks—Sophocles, Euripides, Aeschylus, Aristophanes; followed by the Romans, especially Plautus and Terence; then Shakespeare's thirty-seven plays—comedies, tragedies, histories, romances; tragedies, such as *Phèdre*, by the French playwright Racine, comedies, such as *Tartuffe*, by his countryman Molière; English drama by Richard Brinsley Sheridan (*The Rivals*) and Oscar Wilde (*The Importance of Being Ernest*) and G. B. Shaw (*Arms and the Man, Man and Superman, Major Barbara*); the Norwegian playwright Henrik Ibsen (*A Doll's House, Hedda Gabler, The Master Builder*) and the Swedish dramatist August Strindberg (*The Father, Miss Julie, The Dance of Death*); the German Heinrich von Kleist (*Penthesilia* and *The Broken Pitcher*); the Italian (Sicilian) Luigi Pirandello (*Right You Are, If You Think You Are, Six Characters in Search of an Author, Henry IV*); the German Marxist writer Bertolt Brecht (*The Good Woman of Szechuan, The Caucasian Chalk Circle, Mother Courage and Her Children*); the Romanian modernist Ionesco (*Rhinoceros, The Lesson, The Chairs*), and the Irish writer Samuel Beckett, whose *Endgame* and *Waiting for Godot*, his best-known plays, owe something, in their tragicomic temper and their refusal to provide easy answers to profound questions, to the Russian playwright Anton Chekhov, whose plays continue to enthrall audiences worldwide, especially his last plays, *Uncle Vanya, Three Sisters*, and *The Cherry Orchard*.

Twentieth-century drama continues the tradition and departs from it with an abundance of playwrights worth reading. The following brief list identifies only a handful of the many masterful dramatists writing in the United States, the United Kingdom, and continental Europe. In alphabetical order: Edward Albee, Amiri Baraka, Robert Bolt, Caryl Churchill, Noel Coward, Christopher Durang, T. S. Eliot, Dario Fo, Michael Frayn, Lorraine Hansberry, David Hare, Tony Kushner, Federico García Lorca, Terrence McNally, Arthur Miller, Sean O'Casey, Eugene O'Neill, John Osborne, Harold Pinter, Terence Rattigan, Jean-Paul Sartre, Peter Shaffer, Sam Shepard, Neil Simon, Stephen Sondheim, Tom Stoppard, John Millington Synge, Wendy Wasserstein, Thornton Wilder, Tennessee Williams, and August Wilson—again, among other notable dramatists too numerous to count..

Nor can we overlook the vast array of narrative and lyric poetry written by poets the world over across a variety of languages. Among the earliest of important English poets is Geoffrey Chaucer, whose *Canterbury Tales* have delighted readers for more than six hundred years. As a well-educated fourteenth-century intellectual, the English poet Chaucer was familiar with Latin literature, history, and philosophy. The most important influence on Chaucer's writing, however, was not Latin but Italian. A number of Chaucer's *Canterbury Tales*, as well as the basic narrative structure of the book, derive from Giovanni Boccaccio's *Decameron*, another memorably engaging medieval fictional work, written in the Tuscan dialect (like Dante's *Divine Comedy*). The *Decameron* is a collection of a hundred *novelle*, or short stories, told by ten Florentines, seven women and three men. They tell the stories to pass the time, having escaped plague-infested Florence. Their tales center on the lives and fortunes of ordinary people, with wit and worldly cynicism.

Chaucer died before completing his *Canterbury Tales*, a collection of stories told by a group of pilgrims traveling from London to Canterbury, to worship at the shrine of St. Thomas à Becket, who was murdered on the cathedral altar there. The tales depict medieval figures from the highest to the lowest classes. Chaucer's narrators reveal themselves through the tales they tell, with ironic and satiric portraits of the pilgrims developed through the voice of Chaucer's overall narrator. This "naive" narrator fails to discriminate between good and evil aspects of human motivation and behavior. This narrative incapacity allows Chaucer to use irony as an instrument of satire, as his wit and observation reveal a zest for life from its lowest and bawdiest to its most elegant and spiritual. This kind of complex vision and nuanced narrative perspective move Chaucer well beyond typical medieval modes of storytelling.

You very likely know many of the following lyric poets from an occasional poem rather than from reading an entire book of their poems, or from a reading of their collected or even selected works. Yet that is one way to get to know a poet well—to read his or her work a bit at a time over an extended period, becoming familiar with the poet's style and subjects, his or her persistent preoccupations and ways of handling language. Here are a number of poets whose work you might like to get to know better in this way. They are listed alphabetically rather than chronologically.

Anna Akhmatova, Matthew Arnold, Margaret Atwood, W. H. Auden, Imamu Amiri Baraka, Matsuo Bashō, Charles Baudelaire, Wendell Berry, Elizabeth Bishop, William Blake, Jorge Luis Borges, Anne Bradstreet, Joseph Brodsky, Emily Brontë, Gwendolyn Brooks, Elizabeth Barrett Browning, Robert Browning, Robert Burns, George Gordon, Lord Byron, Thomas Campion, Lewis Carroll, Raymond Carver, C. V. Cavafy, Paul Celan, Lucille Clifton, Samuel Taylor Coleridge, Billy Collins, Stephen Crane, Countee Cullen, E. E. Cummings, Emily Dickinson, H. D. (Hilda Doolittle), John Donne, Mark Doty, Rita Dove, Michael Drayton, John Dryden, Du Fu, Paul Laurence Dunbar, T. S. Eliot, Ralph Waldo Emerson, Donald Finkel, Robert Fitzgerald, Robert Francis, Robert Frost, Allen Ginsberg, Nikki Giovanni, Louise Glück, Robert Graves, Thomas Gray, Donald Hall, Thomas Hardy, Michael Harper, Robert Hayden, Seamus Heaney, George Herbert, Robert Herrick, Michael Hogan, John Hollander, Gerard Manley Hopkins, A. E. Housman, Langston Hughes, Ted Hughes, Kobayashi Issa, Ben Jonson, John Keats, Galway Kinnell, Kenneth Koch, Philip Larkin, D. H. Lawrence, Edward Lear, Giacomo Leopardi, Li Po (Li Bai), Federico García Lorca, Audre Lorde, Richard Lovelace, Amy Lowell, Robert Lowell.

Archibald MacLeish, Stéphane Mallarmé, Osip Mandelstam, Christopher Marlowe, Andrew Marvell, John Masefield, Claude McKay, Peter Meinke, Robert Mezey, Edna St. Vincent Millay, Czesław Miłosz, John Milton, Marianne Moore, Thomas Nashe, Pablo Neruda, Sharon Olds, Mary Oliver, Ovid, Wilfred Owen,

Boris Pasternak, Octavio Paz, Francesco Petrarca (Petrarch), Marge Piercy, Robert Pinsky, Sylvia Plath, Edgar Allan Poe, Alexander Pope, Ezra Pound, Jacques Prévert, Sir Walter Raleigh, John Crowe Ransom, Henry Reed, Alastair Reid, Adrienne Rich, Rainer Maria Rilke, Arthur Rimbaud, Edwin Arlington Robinson, Theodore Roethke, Kraft Rompf, Christina Rossetti, Dante Gabriel Rossetti, Rumi, Kay Ryan, Carl Sandburg, Sappho, Anne Sexton, William Shakespeare, Percy Bysshe Shelley, Sir Philip Sidney, John Skelton, Gary Snyder, Robert Southwell, Edmund Spenser, William Stafford, Wallace Stevens, Mark Strand, Henry Howard, Earl of Surrey, May Swenson, Wisława Szymborska, James Tate, Alfred Lord Tennyson, Dylan Thomas, Chidiock Tichborne, Jean Toomer, John Updike, Paul Valéry, César Vallejo, Paul Verlaine, Robert Wallace, Wang Wei, Walt Whitman, Richard Wilbur, William Carlos Williams, William Wordsworth, James Wright, Thomas Wyatt, William Butler Yeats, Yevgeny Yevtushenko.

Some of the authors and works named here you have, very likely, already read—perhaps before you were ready to appreciate them. If you were lucky, you read them at an age-appropriate time, or, even better, you may have read them a second or third time as an adult. If you haven't, perhaps it's time you should. As Thoreau also remarked about reading: "To read well, that is, to read true books in a true spirit, is a noble exercise, and one that will task the reader. . . . It requires a training such as the athletes underwent, the steady intention almost of the whole life" (403). Thoreau's observation captures the challenge and the opportunity, the work and the pleasure of reading the best works of literature we can find.

The Literary Canon

The previous discussion of literary works outlines, essentially, a canon, a prescribed set of works of literature that are worth reading. The notion of a literary canon or collection of accepted books derives from the idea of a biblical canon—those books accepted officially as "sacred scripture." A scriptural canon contains those

works deemed to represent the moral standards and religious beliefs of a particular group, Jews or Muslims, for whom the Bible and
Koran (or Quran), respectively, are canonical scriptural texts. To
form their canon, Christians add to the Hebrew Bible a number of
other works, including the four Gospels, the Epistles, and the book
of Revelation. For every work accepted into a scriptural canon,
others exist that were not accepted; those works are noncanonical—
works that include the book of Maccabees, which was not included in the Hebrew Bible, and the Gospel of Thomas, which was
omitted from the Christian New Testament.

In the same way, the list of writers and works identified in this
chapter constitutes a canon, with many other literary works omitted. The list could of course be extended with many more writers
and works that are equally worthy and of significant value for readers. Yet even if this were done, there would still be some kinds of
books that serious readers might exclude from such a canonical list.
Much fantasy and science fiction, for example, might not be included (though with some exceptions—for example, J.R.R. Tolkien's *The Lord of the Rings* trilogy, C. S. Lewis's *Chronicles of Narnia*
books, and Philip Pullman's *His Dark Materials* trilogy). What
about the Harry Potter series? And how about Suzanne Collins's
popular dystopian series that includes *The Hunger Games*, *Catching
Fire*, and *Mockingjay*? And what about science fiction books that
promote serious critical and creative thinking about complex
human problems—books such as Isaac Asimov's *I, Robot* and *The
Foundation Trilogy*, Ray Bradbury's *Martian Chronicles* and *Fahren-
heit 451*, Arthur C. Clarke's *Childhood's End* and *2001: A Space
Odyssey*, Ursula K. Le Guin's *The Dispossessed* and *The Left Hand of
Darkness*, and H.G. Wells's *The Time Machine* and *The Invisible Man*,
among many other worthy candidates.

As with fantasy and science fiction, so with detective stories and
novels, western novels, romances, vampire books, and explicitly
religious-based fiction. On the one hand, we might say that these
books don't belong in the canon of serious literature. On the other
hand, however, we might say that certain examples of books from
these genres—the Sherlock Holmes novels and stories, for example, or the works by Le Guin, Tolkien, and Lewis—should be

included for their literary qualities, as well as for the qualities of creative thinking they manifest, and the critical and creative thinking they provoke.

There will always be debate about what books are most worth reading. This is natural and inevitable. Books we consider classics today were not always thought worthy of inclusion in school and university curricula. This was the case for many years with works of American literature, which were largely considered inferior to British literary works. And earlier, works of British literature weren't seen as worthy of inclusion for university study, which focused on classics written in Latin and Greek, relegating English literature to a position of entertainment and "outside reading"—the very place accorded today to many works of the popular genres that fill the ranks of the best-seller lists.

So where does that leave us on the question of what we should read—what is worth reading, and why we might read it? One answer is to find a balance between the popular and the canonical, between accessible works of easy reading and those more challenging and demanding literary works. Samuel Johnson, the magisterial eighteenth-century critic, suggests that we should read only what interests us because in reading what we feel we should rather than what we want, we won't really attend to or be engaged by the work. As a result we won't enjoy it and we won't remember it. Johnson's sentiments are echoed by Alan Jacobs in *The Pleasures of Reading in an Age of Distraction*, in which he argues that we should read according to whim, that is, read just what strikes us as being of interest, what tempts our curiosity. Jacobs agrees with Johnson and argues that seeing reading as a chore can destroy a real interest in and love for reading. Jacobs and others suggest that reading out of a sense of duty—reading certain books because they are somehow "good for you"—is counterproductive.

Jacobs does, however, acknowledge that there are times when we are obliged to read something that we would not have chosen for ourselves—times we are required to read not for pleasure, but for an externally induced purpose—to fulfill an assignment at school or work, for example. He suggests that in those cases we apply ourselves to the task of reading, that we take notes, read actively and responsibly, and that we try to find a node of engagement for this work of reading. He distinguishes this kind of reading, however, from the reading we do for ourselves, for our own pleasure, profit, and multiple purposes. Nonetheless, we may occasionally find that those "required" reading assignments introduce us to books that we find ourselves enjoying, and which we may want to pursue further.

Why We Read Literature

In *The Pleasures of Reading in an Ideological Age*, Robert Alter emphasizes the unique way each of us enjoys the books and other texts we read. Our particular ways of reading, he notes, are not replicable by others (238). Yet he does acknowledge that there is common ground both in the texts we read and in our general ways of approaching them, such that "we can talk to each other, even sometimes persuade each other, about what we read" (238).

In *Seven Pleasures*, Willard Spiegelman describes the pleasures of reading as "the sheer thrill of words, their sounds and half-imagined meanings," along with "the essential reality of its own" that language provides (29). He advocates reading ravenously. Yet he also encourages us to read slowly, with deliberate attention. "Readers are tortoises," he remarks, "not hares" (47). And, finally, he writes that reading is the "source of occasional disturbance, threat, anxiety, and a cause for questions and alarms" (54). Citing the novelist and essayist author of *The Common Reader*, Virginia Woolf, he reminds us that reading is its own reward, its own pleasure.

In an essay titled "Notes toward a Definition of the Ideal Reader," Alberto Manguel describes what ideal readers do. What are some of his characterizations of that ideal reader? "Ideal readers do not follow a story," he writes, "they partake of it. . . . they do not reconstruct a story: they recreate it" (151). Manguel sees the ideal reader as an inventor, who subverts the text, and who does not take the writer's word for granted (196). The ideal reader, thus, exercises power over what he or she reads. The ideal reader is not intimidated by books and authors; instead ideal readers assume authority for themselves, the authority to make what they read their own, even to the point of making every book read part of their individual autobiography.

Like Manguel, Harold Bloom, another master reader, agrees. In *How to Read and Why*, Bloom suggests that individual readers must retain the "capacity to form their judgments and opinions," that they read, essentially, "for themselves" (21). Bloom argues, further, that why readers read must be left to themselves and be directly related to their own interests.

Edward Mendelson supports this view in his book about reading novels, *The Things That Matter*. Mendelson subscribes to a popular but sometimes discredited notion that we read novels to identify with their characters and to learn from them things that are important for our lives—things that matter. He argues that novels provide "models or examples of the kinds of life that a reader might or might not choose to live" (12). We learn about varieties of love, for example, from *Wuthering Heights* and *Mrs. Dalloway*, and we learn about types of marriages—how they can work and how go wrong—from novels such as *Middlemarch*, *To the Lighthouse*, and *Portrait of a Lady*.

We have a responsibility to the literary works we read. Our major responsibility lies in giving them and their authors their due. We need to hear those books and authors out, letting them have their say. This is so whether we agree with an author's views or not, whether a book's ideas are difficult or accessible, regardless of who wrote the it, when it was written, or why. We need, in short, to respect the integrity of the texts we read, not expecting something from a book that it does not intend to provide. When we read a novel, we may hope for a happy ending, but a writer is not obligated to provide one. To criticize the book for lacking that happy ending offends the ethic of reading. And when we read a detective novel or a work of fantasy or science fiction, it is unjust to expect or even demand that it be realistic. Its genre requires that it do and be something other than realistic.

Reading good and great books patiently and deliberately, savoring their language and ideas, is one way to increase our knowledge, deepen our understanding, and develop our minds while also tending to our emotional needs. Good and great and interesting books contribute to our psychic well-being. Setting a goal of reading one such literary work per week, perhaps including a lyric poet and a dramatist each month, might be a good way to enrich your imaginative world while deepening your thinking and adding a degree of pleasure to your life. But remember to follow the advice of Johnson and Jacobs, cited earlier, who suggest that you should read what interests you, what you are hungry for or curious about. Let that be your guiding principle—at least now at the start of some new adventures in literature that await you.

Literature provides us with imagined laboratories in which ethical and unethical action, moral and immoral behavior are tested, places where characters learn to know themselves or contrive ways to avoid self-knowledge. In these and other ways, works of literature serve as encounters with imaginative possibilities, analogues of our lives that reveal us to ourselves and deepen our knowledge of the human comedy in all its multitudinous variety.

Acknowledgments

My first and deepest acknowledgment is to the late Robert Scholes, whose death in 2016 motivated me to revisit notes I had made during an interview with him years before, and to reread half a dozen of his books. The result was this book's second chapter, "Reading for the Truth," the first written and a stimulus for the rest. Scholes, however, provided more than a literary-critical influence; he also inspired me to try to become the kind of exemplary reader and teacher of literature he was. Robert Scholes is alive in my thinking and writing; he has become part of who I am as a reader, writer, and teacher.

Among my best readers and astute critics is my late friend Steve Dunn, who gave parts of the near-final manuscript a scrupulous line edit. The book is better for his having read it with such attention and care.

A number of colleagues read various drafts of the full manuscript or of individual chapters. I am grateful to the following people for their helpful suggestions for revision. The book is better for their having offered wise counsel: Adrian Barlow, David Bartholomae, Anton Borst, Linda Costanzo Cahir, William V. Costanzo, Joan DelFattore, Pat C. Hoy II, César Rodriguez, Larry Scanlon, John Schilb, and Anne Lydia Ward.

I would like to thank my editor, Peter Dougherty, for his faith in me and his interest in this book. He secured thoughtful reviewers and frequently offered additional insights of his own over multiple drafts. Peter also provided the book's title.

Thanks also to Peter's colleagues at Princeton University Press for their expertise in bringing the book into being: to Erin Suydam, my production manager, who steered the project through its multiple phases with grace and skill; to Lauren Lepow, my copyeditor, who saved me from any number of mistakes that I myself overlooked; to Alena Chekanov, for her assistance securing permissions; to Bob Bettendorf and Matt Avery for their respective domains of expertise in providing engaging copy text and an attractive design for the book's jacket; to Pamela L. Schnitter for providing its elegant interior design; to Alyssa Sanford and Kathryn Stevens for their guidance in bringing the book to the attention of prospective readers, reviewers, and course adopters. I have been fortunate indeed in having this first-class team behind this book.

. . .

Finally, I gratefully acknowledge the publishers who have kindly given their permission to publish material in this volume.

- "This Is Just to Say" and "To a Poor Old Woman" by William Carlos Williams (*Collected Poems* Volume I 1909–1939, 2018) are reprinted here by kind permission of Carcanet Press Limited, Manchester, UK.
- James Wright, "A Blessing" from *Above the River: The Complete Poems and Selected Prose*, © 1990 by Anne Wright. Published by Wesleyan University Press and reprinted with permission.
- "Dream Deferred [Harlem 2]" from *The Collected Poems of Langston Hughes* by Langston Hughes, edited by Arnold Rampersad with David Roessel, associate editor, copyright © 1994 by the Estate of Langston Hughes. Used by permission of Alfred A. Knopf, an imprint of the Knopf Doubleday Publishing Group, a division of Penguin Random House LLC. All rights reserved.
- Zen parables "Learning to be Silent" and "Muddy Road" from *Zen Flesh, Zen Bones*, compiled by Paul Reps (Tuttle Publishing, 1998). Copyright © 1957, 1985 Charles E. Tuttle Co., Inc.
- "Archaic Torso of Apollo," translation copyright © 1982 by Stephen Mitchell; from *Selected Poetry of Rainer Maria Rilke* by Rainer Maria Rilke, edited and translated by Stephen Mitchell. Used by permission of Random House, an imprint and division of Penguin Random House LLC. All rights reserved.

References

Alter, Robert. *The Pleasures of Reading in an Ideological Age*. Norton, 1990.

Austen, Jane. *Pride and Prejudice*. Penguin, 2002.

Bacon, Francis. *The Essays*. Penguin, 1986.

Bakewell, Sarah. *How to Live*. Other Press, 2010.

Baldwin, James. *The Fire Next Time*. Vintage, 1992.

———. "Notes of a Native Son." In *Collected Essays*. Library of America, 1998.

Barlow, Adrian. "The Community of Literature." In *Critical Reading across the Curriculum*, vol. 1, *Humanities*, edited by Robert DiYanni and Anton Borst. Wiley-Blackwell, 2017.

———. *World and Time: Teaching Literature in Context*. Cambridge University Press, 2011.

Barthes, Roland. "Day by Day with Roland Barthes." In *On Signs*, edited by Marshall Blonsky. Johns Hopkins University Press, 1985.

———. "Toys." In *Mythologies*. Hill and Wang, 1957.

Beal, Timothy. *The Rise and Fall of the Bible*. Houghton Mifflin Harcourt, 2011.

Birkerts, Sven. *The Gutenberg Elegies*. Farrar, Straus and Giroux, 2006.

———. *Reading Life: Books for the Ages*. Graywolf Press, 2007.

Bishop, Elizabeth. "One Art." *Poems*. Farrar, Straus and Giroux, 2011.

Bloom, Harold. *How to Read and Why*. Scribner, 2001.

Borst, Anton. "A Shared Horizon: Critical Reading and Digital Natives." In *Critical Reading across the Curriculum*, vol. 1, *Humanities*, edited by Robert DiYanni and Anton Borst. Wiley-Blackwell, 2017.

Burke, Kenneth. *Counterstatement*. University of Chicago Press, 1957.

———. *Language as Symbolic Action*. University of California Press, 1966.

———. *The Philosophy of Literary Form*. 3rd ed. University of California Press, 1974.

Butler, Judith. "What Value Do the Humanities Have?" Graduation address, McGill University, May 30, 2013.

Calvino, Italo. *Why Read the Classics?* Mariner Books, 2014.

Carey, John. *What Good Are the Arts?* Oxford University Press, 2010.

Carr, Nicholas. *The Shallows*. Norton, 2011.

Chiasson, Dan. "Reader, I Googled It." *New Yorker*, August 26, 2019.

Coates, Ta-Nehisi. *Between the World and Me*. Spiegel and Grau, 2015.

Cofer, Judith Ortiz. "Casa." In *Silent Dancing*. Arte Publico, 1990.

Davis, Lydia. "The Story Is the Thing: Lucia Berlin's *A Manual for Cleaning Women*." In *Essays One*. Farrar, Straus and Giroux, 2019.

Davis, Philip. *Reading and the Reader*. Oxford University Press, 2014.

de Botton, Alain. *How Proust Can Change Your Life*. Pantheon, 1997.

Dehaene, Stanislas. *Reading in the Brain*. Penguin, 2010.

Didion, Joan. "Los Angeles Notebook." In *We Tell Ourselves Stories in Order to Live: Collected Nonfiction*. Knopf, 2006.

DiYanni, Robert, ed. *Literature: Reading Fiction, Poetry, Drama, and the Essay*. McGraw-Hill, 1986.

DiYanni, Robert, and Anton Borst, eds. *Critical Reading across the Curriculum*. Vol. 1, *Humanities*. Wiley-Blackwell, 2017.

Doyle, Brian. "Joyas Voladoras." *American Scholar* 73, no. 4 (Autumn 2004).

Eaglestone, Robert. *Contemporary Fiction*. Oxford University Press, 2013.

Eagleton, Terry. *The Event of Literature*. Yale University Press, 2013.

Eliot, George. "The Natural History of German Life." CreateSpace, 2016.

Eliot, T. S. *Collected Poems 1909–1962*. Harcourt, Brace & World, 1963.

———. "The Metaphysical Poets." In *Selected Essays of T. S. Eliot*. Harcourt, Brace and World, 1964.

———. "Tradition and the Individual Talent." In *Selected Essays of T. S. Eliot*. Harcourt, Brace, and World, 1964.

Ellison, Ralph. "Living with Music." In *Shadow and Act*. Vintage, 1995.

Emerson, Ralph Waldo. "The American Scholar," "Nature," and "History." In *Essays and Lectures*. Library of America, 1983.

———. *Journals and Miscellaneous Notebooks*. Harvard University Press, 1960–1982.

Epstein, Joseph. "The Bookish Life." *First Things*, November 2018.

———. *A Literary Education and Other Essays*. Axios Press, 2014.

Felski, Rita. *Uses of Literature*. Blackwell, 2008.

Foer, Franklin. *World without End*. Penguin, 2017.

Fowles, John. *The Pleasure of Reading*. Edited by Antonia Fraser. Bloomsbury, 2015.

Frost, Robert. "Mending Wall." In *Collected Poems & Prose*, 776–778. Library of America, 1995.

Frye, Northrop. *The Educated Imagination*. Indiana University Press, 1964.

Gass, William. "In Defense of the Book." *Harper's*, November 1999; October 2018.

Geary, James. *I Is an Other: The Secret Life of Metaphor and How It Shapes the Way We See the World.* Harper Perennial, 2012.

Giraldi, William. *American Audacity.* Liveright, 2018.

Goodman, Ellen. "The Company Man." In *Close to Home.* Simon and Schuster, 1979.

Gornick, Vivian. *Unfinished Business.* Farrar, Straus and Giroux, 2020.

Goulish, Matthew. *39 Microlectures.* Routledge, 2000.

Greene, A. Kendra. "For Eons, Iceland Has Endured Calamity through Books." *Wall Street Journal,* July 16, 2020.

Greene, Kiersten. "Text(ured) Considerations." In *Critical Reading across the Curriculum,* vol. 2, *Social and Natural Sciences,* edited by Anton Borst and Robert DiYanni. Wiley-Blackwell, 2020.

Hales, Dianne. *La Bella Lingua.* Broadway Books, 2010.

Hamlin, Amy. "Approaching Intellectual Emancipation: Critical Reading in Art, Art History, and Wikipedia." In *Critical Reading across the Curriculum,* vol. 1, *Humanities,* edited by Robert DiYanni and Anton Borst. Wiley-Blackwell, 2017.

Hayles, N. Katherine. "How We Read: Hyper, Close, Machine." *ADE Bulletin* no. 150, 2010.

Hemingway, Ernest. *A Moveable Feast: The Restored Edition.* Scribner, 2010.

Hoagland, Edward. *The Tugman's Passage.* Random House, 1982.

Hoy, Pat C. II. "Reading and Writing: Reciprocal Acts." In *Critical Reading across the Curriculum,* vol. 1, *Humanities,* edited by Robert DiYanni and Anton Borst. Wiley-Blackwell, 2017.

Hughes, Langston. "Dream Deferred." In *The Panther and the Lash.* Random House, 1951.

———. "Salvation." In *The Big Sea.* Hill and Wang, 1940.

Hurston, Zora Neale. "How It Feels to Be Colored Me." *The World Tomorrow,* May 1928.

Iser, Wolfgang. *The Act of Reading.* Johns Hopkins University Press, 1980.

———. *How to Do Theory.* Blackwell, 2006.

———. *The Implied Reader.* Johns Hopkins University Press, 1978

Jacobs, Alan. *The Pleasures of Reading in an Age of Distraction.* Oxford University Press, 2011.

James, Henry. *Theory of Fiction.* Edited by James E. Miller, Jr. University of Nebraska Press, 1972.

Johnson, Samuel. *Major Works.* Oxford University Press, 2009.

Joyce, James. *Dubliners.* Edited by Terence Brown. Centennial Edition, Viking, 2014.

———. *Selected Letters of James Joyce*. Edited by Richard Ellmann. Faber and Faber, 1975.

Kaufman, Andrew D. *Give War and Peace a Chance*. Simon & Schuster, 2014.

Keats, John. *Complete Poems*. Edited by Jack Stillinger. Harvard University Press, 1978.

Kendall, Tim. *The Art of Robert Frost*. Yale University Press, 2013.

Kenko, Yoshida. *Essays in Idleness*. Translated by Donald Greene. Tuttle, 1981.

Klinkenborg, Verlyn. "Books to Have and to Hold." *New York Times*, August 11, 2013.

Lawrence, D. H. *Studies in Classic American Literature*. Penguin, 1990.

Leith, Sam. *Words like Loaded Pistols: Rhetoric from Aristotle to Obama*. Basic Books, 2012.

Lesser, Wendy. *Why I Read*. Farrar, Straus and Giroux, 2014.

Lewis, C. S. *The Reading Life*. HarperCollins, 2019.

Luzzi, Joseph. *In a Dark Wood*. Harper, 2015.

Manguel, Alberto. *A Reader on Reading*. Yale University Press, 2010.

Mead, Rebecca. *My Life in Middlemarch*, Crown, 2014.

Melville, Herman. *The Confidence Man*. Dover, 2017.

———. *Moby-Dick*. Library of America, 1983.

Mendelsohn, Daniel. *An Odyssey*. Knopf, 2017.

Mendelson, Edward. *The Things That Matter*. Pantheon, 2006.

Mikics, David. *Slow Reading in a Hurried Age*. Harvard University Press, 2013.

Montaigne, Michel. *The Complete Essays of Montaigne*. Translated by Donald Frame. Stanford University Press, 1957.

Moran, Joe. "A Pedant's Apology." In *First You Write a Sentence*. Viking, 2018.

Newkirk, Thomas. *The Art of Slow Reading*. Heinemann, 2012.

———. *Minds Made for Stories*. Heinemann, 2014.

O'Connor, Flannery. *Collected Works*. Library of America, 1988.

Olney, James. *Metaphors of Self*. Princeton University Press, 1972.

Orwell, George. "Shooting an Elephant," "Some Thoughts on the Common Toad." In *Essays*. Knopf, 2002.

Price, Leah. *What We Talk about When We Talk about Books*. Basic Books, 2019.

Reps, Paul. Compiler. *Zen Flesh, Zen Bones*. Tuttle, 1998.

Richardson, Robert D., ed. *First We Read, Then We Write: Emerson on the Creative Process*. University of Iowa Press, 2009.

Rilke, Rainer Maria. *The Selected Poetry of Rainer Maria Rilke.* Translated by Stephen Mitchell. Vintage, 1989.

Robinson, Marilynne. "The Brain Is Larger than the Sea." In *Light the Dark*, edited by Joe Fassler. Penguin, 2017.

Russo, Richard. "The Lives of Others." *Harper's Magazine*, June 2020.

Savarese, Ralph James. *Read It Feelingly.* Duke University Press, 2019.

Scholes, Robert. *Protocols of Reading.* Yale University Press, 1989.

———. *Textual Power.* Yale University Press, 1985.

Schwalbe, Will. *Books for Living.* Random House, 2016.

———. *The End of Your Life Book Club.* Vintage, 2013.

Scott, A. O. *Better Living through Criticism.* Penguin, 2016.

Seneca. *On the Shortness of Life.* Translated by John W. Basore. GLH Publishing, 2016.

Shakespeare, William. *The Tragedy of Julius Caesar.* In *The Riverside Shakespeare*, edited by G. Blakemore Evans et al. 2nd ed. Houghton Mifflin, 1997.

Shaw, Prue. *Reading Dante: From Here to Eternity.* Liveright, 2014.

Smiley, Jane. "Nobody Asked You to Write That Novel." In *Light the Dark*, edited by Joe Fassler. Penguin, 2017.

Smith, Ali. *Artful.* Penguin, 2014.

Smith, Zadie. *Feel Free.* Penguin, 2018.

Solnit, Rebecca. Introduction to *The Best American Essays 2019.* Mariner Books, 2019.

———. *Men Explain Things to Me.* Haymarket Books, 2014.

Sontag, Susan. "A Woman's Beauty: Put Down or Power Source." In *Sontag: Essays of the 1960s & 1970s.* Library of America, 2013.

Spiegelman, Willard. *Seven Pleasures.* Farrar, Straus and Giroux, 2009.

Thoreau, Henry David. *The Journal of Henry David Thoreau, 1837–1861.* New York Review Books Classics, 2009.

———. *Walden and Civil Disobedience.* Viking/Library of America, 1854/1983.

Tompkins, Jane. *Reading through the Night.* University of Virginia Press, 2018.

Turner, Mark. *The Literary Mind.* Oxford University Press, 1998.

Twain, Mark. *Adventures of Huckleberry Finn.* In *Mississippi Writings.* Viking/Library of America, 1982.

Walker, Alice. "In Search of Our Mothers' Gardens." In *In Search of Our Mothers' Gardens.* Harcourt, Brace Jovanovich, 1983.

Watson, Cecilia. *Semicolon.* Ecco, 2019.

White, E. B. "Moonwalk," Notes and Comment. *New Yorker*, July 26, 1969. © Conde Nast.

Whitehead, Colson. "City Limits." In *The Colossus of New York*. Anchor, 2004.

Whitman, Walt. *Poems and Prose*. Library of America, 1982.

Williams, William Carlos. *Selected Poems*. New Directions, 1985.

Wills, Gary. *Rome and Rhetoric: Shakespeare's "Julius Caesar."* Yale University Press, 2011.

Wimmers, Inge. *Poetics of Reading*. Princeton University Press, 1988.

Winterson, Jeanette. *The Pleasure of Reading*. Edited by Antonia Fraser. Bloomsbury, 2015.

Wolf, Maryanne. *Proust and the Squid*. Harper, 2008.

———. *Reader, Come Home*. Harper, 2018.

Wood, James. *The Nearest Thing to Life*. Brandeis University Press, 2015.

Wood, Michael. *Literature and the Taste of Knowledge*. Cambridge University Press, 2005.

Woolf, Virginia. "George Eliot." In *Essays of Virginia Woolf*, vol. 4, *1925–1928*. Houghton Mifflin Harcourt, 1994.

———. *Selected Essays*. Oxford University Press, 2009.

Wordsworth, William. Preface to *Lyrical Ballads*. In *Lyrical Ballads*, edited by F. Stafford. Oxford University Press, 1802/2013.

———. *Poetical Works*, edited by Thomas Hutchinson and Ernest De Selincourt. Oxford University Press, 1904/1974.

Wright, James. *Collected Poems*. Wesleyan University Press, 2007.

Yeats, William Butler. *The Collected Poems of W. B. Yeats*. Edited by Richard Finneran. Rev. 2nd ed. Scribner, 1996.

Index

www.ingramcontent.com/pod-product-compliance
Ingram Content Group UK Ltd.
Pitfield, Milton Keynes, MK11 3LW, UK
UKHW042124100125
453448UK00004B/237